THE EMOTIONS

BY

CARL GEORG LANGE (1834–1900)
University of Copenhagen

AND

WILLIAM JAMES (1842–1910)
Harvard University

(Facsimile of 1922 Edition)

HAFNER PUBLISHING COMPANY
New York and London
1967

Originally published 1922
Reprinted 1967, by arrangement
with Williams & Wilkins Company

Printed and published by
HAFNER PUBLISHING COMPANY, INC.
31 East 10th Street
New York, N.Y. 10003

Library of Congress Catalog Card No.: 67-20562

Printed in U.S.A. by
NOBLE OFFSET PRINTERS, INC.
NEW YORK 3, N. Y.

CONTENTS

EDITOR'S PREFACE

The publication, in 1872, of Darwin's *The Expression of the Emotions in Man and Animals* had a profound effect upon the development of Psychology. Darwin's book gave to three men the impetus to develop the theory of the emotions as organic processes, and this theory has not only become so strongly entrenched in scientific thought that it is practically assumed today as the basis for the study of the emotional life, but has also led to the development of the hypothesis of reaction or response as the basis of all mental life: a hypothesis which is rapidly supplanting the phrenologists' theory of brain-activity.

The three men who independently developed the organic theory of the emotions were Carl Georg Lange in Denmark, William James in America, and Alexander Sutherland in Australia. The writings of James and Lange had profound influence on contemporary and later psychologists, and on this account it is not unfair to apply the name "James-Lange Theory" to the organic theory of the emotions, as is customarily done. This implies no lack of appreciation of the work of Sutherland, or of the contributions of Ribot, Mosso, and later investigators.

We present in this volume a new translation of Lange's *Ueber Gemüthsbewegungen*, made by Miss Istar A. Haupt from Kurella's German version: together with a reprinting of James' *What is an Emotion?* and his chapter on "The Emotions" from the *Principles of Psychology*. These important foundations of modern psychology are thus made readily accessible to students of psychology, philosophy, and physiology; and a real need is served.

In the chapter in the *Principles*, James repeated some of the material which had already been presented in the *Mind* article. It has however been deemed advisable to reprint the earlier article as well as the chapter. Historical considerations alone would warrant this, since the chapter is based both on the article and upon Lange's monograph, and it is important to have these two independent foundations presented side by side. But there is a still

5

more important reason, in that the *Mind* article gives a much more clear-cut presentation of the organic theory of the emotions than does the chapter from the *Principles:* and in the latter James concedes much more to the esthetic and spiritual emotions in the way of independence of somatic and visceral processes than he does in the former. Whatever may have caused James to soften his views on this point, his first formulation of the theory is in this respect the more important.

Carl (or Karl) Georg Lange was born at Vordingborg, Zealand, Denmark, in 1834. He studied medicine at the University of Copenhagen, and received his degree in 1859. In 1877 he was made Professor of Pathological Anatomy in the same University and held that position until his death in 1900. He was a man of eminence in the field of medicine, but his monograph on the emotions is by far his greatest achievement.

William James was born in New York City in 1842, and graduated from Harvard in medicine in 1872. His interests even then were in psychology and philosophy rather than in medicine, and although his first university appointment, in 1872, was as Lecturer in Physiology in the Harvard Department of Natural History, he expressed a strong preference for a position in philosophy then vacant. His poor health, however, prevented his attempting to secure the latter position.

James' first academic duty was to assist in a course in Physiology and Hygiene given to undergraduates: but in 1876 he offered a course in Physiological Psychology, and organized a psychological laboratory. The following year, the course was transferred to the Department of Philosophy. By later appointments, James was successively made Assistant Professor of Philosophy (1880), Professor of Philosophy (1885), Professor of Psychology (1889), and again Professor of Philosophy (1897). He died in 1910.

Lange's monograph appeared (in Danish) in 1885. A German translation by Dr. Kurella appeared in 1887, and from this Georges Dumas made in 1895 a French translation which ran through several editions. So far as we know, no English translation has been published. James' article appeared in *Mind* in 1884, and his *Principles of Psychology* in 1893. Sutherland's *Origin and Growth of the Moral Instinct* was printed in 1898, but he had formulated his version of the organic theory of the emotions, presented in that book, some time earlier, apparently before reading either James or Lange. We have not deemed it expedient to reprint Sutherland's chapters at this time.

The translation of Lange's monograph was not made from the Danish original, but from Kurella's version, published by Theodor Thomas (Leipzic), and compared with the French text.

For permission to print James' *Mind* article we are indebted to the editor of that journal, and for permission to reprint the chapter of the *Principles*, to Henry Holt and Company.

KNIGHT DUNLAP.

The Johns Hopkins University
March 4, 1922

WHAT IS AN EMOTION?

BY

WILLIAM JAMES

WHAT IS AN EMOTION?

WILLIAM JAMES

[*Mind*, 1884, vol. IX, pp. 188–205]

The physiologists who, during the past few years, have been so
industriously exploring the functions of the brain, have limited
their attempts at explanation to its cognitive and volitional performances. Dividing the brain into sensorial and motor centers,
they have found their division to be exactly paralleled by the
analysis made by empirical psychology, of the perceptive and
volitional parts of the mind into their simplest elements. But
the *æsthetic* sphere of the mind, its longings, its pleasures and
pains, and its emotions, have been so ignored in all these researches
that one is tempted to suppose that if either Dr. Ferrier or Dr.
Munk were asked for a theory in brain-terms of the latter mental
facts, they might both reply, either that they had as yet bestowed
no thought upon the subject, or that they had found it so difficult
to make distinct hypotheses, that the matter lay for them among
the problems of the future, only to be taken up after the simpler
ones of the present should have been definitely solved.

And yet it is even now certain that of two things concerning the
emotions, one must be true. Either separate and special centers
affected to them alone, are their brain-seat, or else they correspond
to processes occurring in the motor and sensory centers, already
assigned, or in others like them, not yet mapped out. If the former be the case we must deny the current view, and hold the
cortex to be something more than the surface of "projection" for
every sensitive spot and every muscle in the body. If the latter
be the case, we must ask whether the emotional "process" in the
sensory or motor center be an altogether peculiar one, or whether
it resembles the ordinary perceptive processes of which those
centers are already recognized to be the seat. The purpose of the
following pages is to show that the last alternative comes nearest
to the truth, and that the emotional brain-processes not only

11

resemble the ordinary sensorial brain-processes, but in very truth *are* nothing but such processes variously combined. The main result of this will be to simplify our notions of the possible complications of brain-physiology, and to make us see that we have already a brain-scheme in our hands whose applications are much wider than its authors dreamed. But although this seems to be the chief result of the arguments I am to urge, I should say that they were not originally framed for the sake of any such result. They grew out of fragmentary introspective observations, and it was only when these had already combined into a theory that the thought of the simplification the theory might bring to cerebral physiology occurred to me, and made it seem more important than before.

I should say first of all that the only emotions I propose expressly to consider here are those that have a distinct bodily expression. That there are feelings of pleasure and displeasure, of interest and excitement, bound up with mental operations, but having no obvious bodily expression for their consequence, would, I suppose, be held true by most readers. Certain arrangements of sounds, of lines, of colours, are agreeable, and others the reverse, without the degree of the feeling being sufficient to quicken the pulse or breathing, or to prompt to movements of either the body or the face. Certain sequences of ideas charm us as much as others tire us. It is a real intellectual delight to get a problem solved, and a real intellectual torment to have to leave it unfinished. The first set of examples, the sounds, lines, and colours are either bodily sensations, or the images of such. The second set seem to depend on processes in the ideational centers exclusively. Taken together, they appear to prove that there are pleasures and pains inherent in certain forms of nerve-action as such, wherever that action occur. The case of these feelings we will at present leave entirely aside, and confine our attention to the more complicated cases in which a wave of bodily disturbance of some kind accompanies the perception of the interesting sights or sounds, or the passage of the exciting train of ideas. Surprise, curiosity, rapture, fear, anger, lust, greed, and the like, become then the names of the mental states with which the person is possessed. The bodily disturbances are said to be the "manifestation" of these several emotions, their "expression" or "natural language;" and these emotions themselves, being so strongly characterised both from within and without, may be called the *standard* emotions.

Our natural way of thinking about these standard emotions is that the mental perception of some fact excites the mental affection called the emotion, and that this latter state of mind gives rise to the bodily expression. My thesis on the contrary is that *the bodily changes follow directly the PERCEPTION of the exciting fact, and that our feeling of the same changes as they occur IS the emotion.* Common sense says, we lose our fortune, are sorry and weep; we meet a bear, are frightened and run; we are insulted by a rival, are angry and strike. The hypothesis here to be defended says that this order of sequence is incorrect, that the one mental state is not immediately induced by the other, that the bodily manifestations must first be interposed between, and that the more rational statement is that we feel sorry because we cry, angry because we strike, afraid because we tremble, and not that we cry, strike, or tremble, because we are sorry, angry, or fearful as the case may be. Without the bodily states following on the perception, the latter would be purely cognitive in form, pale, colourless, destitute of emotional warmth. We might then see the bear, and judge it best to run, receive the insult and deem it right to strike, but we could not actually *feel* afraid or angry.

Stated in this crude way, the hypothesis is pretty sure to meet with immediate disbelief. And yet neither many nor far-fetched considerations are required to mitigate its paradoxical character, and possibly to produce conviction of its truth.

To begin with, readers of the Journal do not need to be reminded that the nervous system of every living thing is but a bundle of predispositions to react in particular ways upon the contact of particular features of the environment. As surely as the hermit-crab's abdomen presupposes the existence of empty whelk-shells somewhere to be found, so surely do the hound's olfactories imply the existence, on the one hand, of deer's or foxes' feet, and on the other, the tendency to follow up their tracks. The neural machinery is but a hyphen between determinate arrangements of matter outside the body and determinate impulses to inhibition or discharge within its organs. When the hen sees a white oval object on the ground she cannot leave it; she must keep upon it and return to it, until at last its transformation into a little mass of moving chirping down elicits from her machinery an entirely new set of performances. The love of man for woman, or of the human mother for her babe, our wrath at snakes and our fear of precipices, may all be described similarly, as instances of the way in which peculiarly conformed pieces of the world's furniture will fatally call forth most particular mental and bodily reactions, in advance of, and often in direct opposition to, the verdict of our deliberate reason concerning them. The labours of Darwin and his successors are only just beginning to reveal the universal parasitism of each special creature upon other special things, and the way in which each creature brings the signature of its special relations stamped on its nervous system with it upon the scene.

Every living creature is in fact a sort of lock, whose wards and springs presuppose special forms of keys, which keys however are not born attached to the locks, but are sure to be found in the world near by as life goes on. And the locks are indifferent to any but their own keys. The egg fails to fascinate the hound, the bird does not fear the precipice, the snake waxes not wroth at his kind, the deer cares nothing for the woman or the human babe. Those who wish for a full development of this point of view, should read Schneider's *Der thierische Wille*—no other book shows how accurately anticipatory are the actions of animals, of the specific features of the environment in which they are to live.

Now among these nervous anticipations are of course to be reckoned the emotions, so far as these may be called forth directly by the perception of certain facts. In advance of all experience of elephants no child can but be frightened if he suddenly finds one trumpeting and charging upon him. No woman can see a handsome little naked baby without delight, no man in the wilderness see a human form in the distance without excitement and curiosity. I said I should consider these emotions only so far as they have bodily movements of some sort for their accompaniments. But my first point is to show that their bodily accompaniments are much more far-reaching and complicated than we ordinarily suppose.

In the earlier books on Expression, written mostly from the artistic point of view, the signs of emotion visible from without were the only ones taken account of. Sir Charles Bell's celebrated *Anatomy of Expression* noticed the respiratory changes; and Bain's and Darwin's treatises went more thoroughly still into the study of the visceral factors involved,—changes in the functioning of glands and muscles, and in that of the circulatory apparatus. But not even a Darwin has exhaustively enumerated *all* the bodily affections characteristic of any one of the standard emotions. More and more, as physiology advances, we begin to discern how almost infinitely numerous and subtle they must be. The researches of Mosso with the plethysmograph have shown that not only the heart, but the entire circulatory system, forms a sort of sounding-board, which every change of our consciousness, however slight, may make reverberate. Hardly a sensation comes to us without sending waves of alternate constriction and dilatation down the arteries of our arms. The blood-vessels of the abdomen act reciprocally with those of the more outward parts. The bladder and bowels, the glands of the mouth, throat, and skin, and the liver, are known to be affected gravely in certain severe emotions, and are unquestionably affected transiently when the emotions are of a lighter sort. That the heart-beats and the rhythm of breathing play a leading part in all emotions whatsoever, is a matter too notorious for proof. And what is really equally prominent, but less likely to be admitted until special attention is drawn to the fact, is the continuous coöperation of the voluntary muscles in our emotional states. Even when no change of outward attitude is produced, their inward tension alters to suit each varying mood, and is felt as a difference of tone or of strain. In depression the flexors tend to prevail; in elation or belligerent excitement the extensors take the lead. And the various permutations and combinations of which these organic activities are susceptible make it abstractly possible that no shade of emotion, however slight, should be without a bodily reverberation as unique, when taken in its totality, as is the mental mood itself.

The immense number of parts modified in each emotion is what makes it so difficult for us to reproduce in cold blood the total and integral expression of any one of them. We may catch the trick with the voluntary muscles, but fail with the skin, glands, heart, and other viscera. Just as an artificially imitated sneeze lacks something of the reality, so the attempt to imitate an emotion in the absence of its normal instigating cause is apt to be rather "hollow."

The next thing to be noticed is this, that every one of the bodily changes, whatsoever it be, is *felt*, acutely or obscurely, the moment it occurs. If the reader has never paid attention to this matter, he will be both interested and astonished to learn how many different local bodily feelings he can detect in himself as characteristic of his various emotional moods. It would be perhaps too much to expect him to arrest the tide of any strong gust of passion for the sake of any such curious analysis as this; but he can observe more tranquil states, and that may be assumed here to be true of the greater which is shown to be true of the less. Our whole cubic capacity is sensibly alive; and each morsel of it contributes its pulsations of feeling, dim or sharp, pleasant, painful, or dubious, to that sense of personality that everyone of us unfailingly carries with him. It is surprising what little items give accent to these complexes of sensibility. When worried by any slight trouble, one may find that the focus of one's bodily consciousness is the contraction, often quite inconsiderable, of the eyes and brows. When momentarily embarrassed, it is something in the pharynx that compels either a swallow, a clearing of the throat, or a slight cough; and so on for as many more instances as might be named. Our concern here being with the general view rather than with the details, I will not linger to discuss these but, assuming the point admitted that every change that occurs must be felt, I will pass on.[1]

---

[1] Of course the physiological question arises, *how* are the changes felt?— *after* they are produced, by the sensory nerves of the organs bringing back to the brain a report of the modifications that have occurred? or *before* they are produced, by our being conscious of the outgoing nerve-currents starting on their way downward towards the parts they are to excite? I believe all the evidence we have to be in favour of the former alternative. The question is too minute for discussion here, but I have said something about it in a paper entitled The Feeling of Effort, in the *Anniversary Memoirs of the Boston Natural History Society*, 1880 (translated in *La Critique Philosophique* for that year, and summarized in *Mind* XX., 582). See also G. E. Müller's *Grundlegung der Psychophysik*, §110.

I now proceed to urge the vital point of my whole theory, which is this. If we fancy some strong emotion, and then try to abstract from our consciousness of it all the feelings of its characteristic bodily symptoms, we find we have nothing left behind, no "mind-stuff" out of which the emotion can be constituted, and that a cold and neutral state of intellectual perception is all that remains. It is true that although most people, when asked, say that their introspection verifies this statement, some persist in saying theirs does not. Many cannot be made to understand the question. When you beg them to imagine away every feeling of laughter and of tendency to laugh from their consciousness of the ludicrousness of an object, and then to tell you what the feeling of of its ludicrousness would be like, whether it be anything more than the perception that the object belongs to the class "funny," they persist in replying that the thing proposed is a physical impossibility, and that they always *must* laugh, if they see a funny object. Of course the task proposed is not the practical one of seeing a ludicrous object and annihilating one's tendency to laugh. It is the purely speculative one of subtracting certain elements of feeling from an emotional state supposed to exist in its fulness, and saying what the residual elements are. I cannot help thinking that all who rightly apprehend this problem will agree with the proposition above laid down. What kind of an emotion of fear would be left, if the feelings neither of quickened heart-beats nor of shallow breathing, neither of trembling lips nor of weakened limbs, neither of goose-flesh nor of visceral stirrings, were present, it is quite impossible to think. Can one fancy the state of rage and picture no ebullition of it in the chest, no flushing of the face, no dilatation of the nostrils, no clenching of the teeth, no impulse to vigorous action, but in their stead limp muscles, calm breathing, and a placid face? The present writer, for one, certainly cannot. The rage is as completely evaporated as the sensation of its so-called manifestations, and the only thing that can possibly be supposed to take its place is some cold-blooded and dispassionate judicial sentence, confined entirely to the intellectual realm, to the effect that a certain person or persons merit chastisement for their sins. In like manner of grief: what would it be without its tears, its sobs, its suffocation of the heart, its pang in the breast-bone?

A feelingless cognition that certain circumstances are deplorable, and nothing more. Every passion in turn tells the same story. A purely disembodied human emotion is a nonentity. I do not say that it is a contradiction in the nature of things, or that pure spirits are necessarily condemned to cold intellectual lives; but I say that for *us*, emotion dissociated from all bodily feeling is inconceivable. The more closely I scrutinise my states, the more persuaded I become, that whatever moods, affections, and passions I have, are in very truth constituted by, and made up of, those bodily changes we ordinarily call their expression or consequence; and the more it seems to me that if I were to become corporeally anaesthetic, I should be excluded from the life of the affections, harsh and tender alike, and drag out an existence of merely cognitive or intellectual form. Such an existence, although it seems to have been the ideal of ancient sages, is too apathetic to be keenly sought after by those born after the revival of the worship of sensibility, a few generations ago.

But if the emotion is nothing but the feeling of the reflex bodily effects of what we call its "object," effects due to the connate adaptation of the nervous system to that object, we seem immediately faced by this objection: most of the objects of civilised man's emotions are things to which it would be preposterous to suppose their nervous systems connately adapted. Most occasions of shame and many insults are purely conventional, and vary with the social environment. The same is true of many matters of dread and of desire, and of many occasions of melancholy and regret. In these cases, at least, it would seem that the ideas of shame, desire, regret, etc., must first have been attached by education and association to these conventional objects before the bodily changes could possibly be awakened. And if in *these* cases the bodily changes follow the ideas, instead of giving rise to them, why not then in all cases?

To discuss thoroughly this objection would carry us deep into the study of purely intellectual Æsthetics. A few words must here suffice. We will say nothing of the argument's failure to distinguish between the idea of an emotion and the emotion itself. We will only recall the well-known evolutionary principle that when a certain power has once been fixed in an animal by virtue of its utility in presence of certain features of the environment, it may turn out to be useful in presence of other features of the environment that had originally nothing to do with either producing or preserving it. A nervous tendency to discharge being once there, all sorts of unforeseen things may pull the trigger and let loose the effects. That among these things should be conventionalities of man's contriving is a matter of no psychological consequence whatever. The most important part of my environment is my fellow-man. The consciousness of his attitude towards me is the perception that normally unlocks most of my shames and indignations and fears. The extraordinary sensitiveness of this consciousness is shown by the bodily modifications wrought in us by the awareness that our fellow-man is noticing us *at all*. No one can walk across the platform at a public meeting with just the same muscular innervation he uses to walk across his room at home. No one can give a message to such a meeting without organic excitement. "Stage-fright" is only the extreme degree of that wholly irrational personal self-consciousness which everyone gets in some measure, as soon as he feels the eyes of a number of strangers fixed upon him, even though he be inwardly convinced that their feeling towards him is of no practical account.[2] This being so, it is not surprising that the additional persuasion that my fellow-man's attitude means either well or ill for me should awaken stronger emotions still. In primitive societies "well" may mean handing me a piece of beef, and "ill" may mean aiming a blow at my skull. In our "cultured age," "ill" may mean cutting me in the street, and "well," giving me an honorary degree. What the action itself may be is quite insignificant, so long as I can perceive in it intent or *animus*. *That* is the emotion-arousing perception; and may give rise to as strong bodily convulsions in me, a civilised man experiencing the treatment of an artificial society, as in any savage prisoner of war,

---

[2] Let it be noted in passing that this personal self-consciousness seems an altogether bodily affair, largely a consciousness of our attitude, and that, like other emotions, it reacts on its physical condition, and leads to modifications of the attitude,—to a certain rigidity in most men, but in children to a regular twisting and squirming fit, and in women to various gracefully shy poses.

learning whether his captors are about to eat him or to make him a member of their tribe.

But now, this objection disposed of, there arises a more general doubt. Is there any evidence, it may be asked, for the assumption that particular perceptions *do* produce widespread bodily effects by a sort of immediate physical influence, antecedent to the arousal of an emotion or emotional idea?

The only possible reply is, that there is most assuredly such evidence. In listening to poetry, drama, or heroic narrative, we are often surprised at the cutaneous shiver which like a sudden wave flows over us, and at the heart-swelling and the lachrymal effusion that unexpectedly catch us at intervals. In listening to music, the same is even more strikingly true. If we abruptly see a dark moving form in the woods, our heart stops beating, and we catch our breath instantly and before any articulate idea of danger can arise. If our friend goes near to the edge of a precipice, we get the well-known feeling of "all-overishness," and we shrink back, although we positively *know* him to be safe, and have no distinct imagination of his fall. The writer well remembers his astonishment, when a boy of seven or eight, at fainting when he saw a horse bled. The blood was in a bucket, with a stick in it, and, if memory does not deceive him, he stirred it round and saw it drip from the stick with no feeling save that of childish curiosity. Suddenly the world grew black before his eyes, his ears began to buzz, and he knew no more. He had never heard of the sight of blood producing faintness or sickness, and he had so little repugnance to it, and so little apprehension of any other sort of danger from it, that even at that tender age, as he well remembers, he could not help wondering how the mere physical presence of a pailful of crimson fluid could occasion in him such formidable bodily effects.

Imagine two steel knife-blades with their keen edges crossing each other at right angles, and moving to and fro. Our whole nervous organisation is "on-edge" at the thought; and yet what emotion can be there except the unpleasant nervous feeling itself, or the dread that more of it may come? The entire fund and capital of the emotion here is the senseless bodily effect the blades immediately arouse. This case is typical of a class: where an ideal emotion seems to precede the bodily symptoms, it is often nothing but a representation of the symptoms themselves. One who has already fainted at the sight of blood may witness the preparations for a surgical operation with uncontrollable heart-sinking and anxiety. He anticipates certain feelings, and the anticipation precipitates their arrival. I am told of a case of morbid terror, of which the subject confessed that what possessed her seemed, more than anything, to be the fear of fear itself. In the various forms of what Professor Bain calls "tender emotion," although the appropriate object must usually be directly contemplated before the emotion can be aroused, yet sometimes thinking of the symptoms of the emotion itself may have the same effect. In sentimental natures, the thought of "yearning" will produce real "yearning." And, not to speak of coarser examples, a mother's imagination of the caresses she bestows on her child may arouse a spasm of parental longing.

In such cases as these, we see plainly how the emotion both begins and ends with what we call its effects or manifestations. It has no mental *status* except as either the presented feeling, or the idea, of the manifestations; which latter thus constitute its entire material, its sum and substance, and its stock-in-trade. And these cases ought to make us see how in all cases the feeling of the manifestations may play a much deeper part in the constitution of the emotion than we are wont to suppose.

If our theory be true, a necessary corollary of it ought to be that any voluntary arousal of the so-called manifestations of a special emotion ought to give us the emotion itself. Of course in the majority of emotions, this test is inapplicable; for many of the manifestations are in organs over which we have no volitional control. Still, within the limits in which it can be verified, experience fully corroborates this test. Everyone knows how panic is increased by flight, and how the giving way to the symptoms of grief or anger increases those passions themselves. Each fit of sobbing makes the sorrow more acute, and calls forth another fit stronger still, until at last repose only ensues with lassitude and with the apparent exhaustion of the machinery. In rage, it is notorious how we "work ourselves up" to a climax by repeated outbreaks of expression. Refuse to express a passion, and it dies. Count ten before venting your anger, and its occasion seems ridiculous. Whistling to keep up courage is no mere figure of speech. On the other hand, sit all day in a moping posture, sigh, and reply to everything with a dismal voice, and your melancholy lingers. There is no more valuable precept in moral education than this, as all who have experience know: if we wish to conquer undesirable emotional tendencies in ourselves, we must assiduously, and in the first instance cold-bloodedly, go through the *outward motions* of those contrary dispositions we prefer to cultivate. The reward of persistency will infallibly come, in the fading out of the sullenness or depression, and the advent of real cheerfulness and kindliness in their stead. Smooth the brow, brighten the eye, contract the dorsal rather than the ventral aspect of the frame, and speak in a major key, pass the genial compliment, and your heart must be frigid indeed if it does not gradually thaw!

The only exceptions to this are apparent, not real. The great emotional expressiveness and mobility of certain persons often lead us to say "They would feel more if they talked less." And in another class of persons, the explosive energy with which passion manifests itself on critical occasions, seems correlated with the way in which they bottle it up during the intervals. But these are only eccentric types of character, and within each type the law of the last paragraph prevails. The sentimentalist is so constructed that "gushing" is his or her normal mode of expression. Putting a stopper on the "gush" will only to a limited extent cause more "real" activities to take its place; in the main it will simply produce listlessness. On the other hand the ponderous and bilious "slumbering volcano," let him repress the expression of his passions as he will, will find them expire if they get no vent at all; whilst if the rare occasions multiply which he deems worthy of their outbreak, he will find them grow in intensity as life proceeds.

I feel persuaded there is no real exception to the law. The formidable effects of suppressed tears might be mentioned, and the calming results of speaking out your mind when angry and having done with it. But these are also but specious wanderings from the rule. Every perception must lead to *some* nervous result. If this be the normal emotional expression, it soon expends itself, and in the natural course of things a calm succeeds. But if the normal issue be blocked from any cause, the currents may under certain circumstances invade other tracts, and there work different and worse effects. Thus vengeful brooding may replace a burst of indignation; a dry heat may consume the frame of one who fain would weep, or he may, as Dante says, turn to stone within; and then tears or a storming-fit may bring a grateful relief. When we teach children to repress their emotions, it is not that they may *feel* more; quite the reverse. It is that they may *think* more; for to a certain extent whatever nerve-currents are diverted from the regions below, must swell the activity of the thought-tracts of the brain.[3]

The last great argument in favour of the priority of the bodily symptoms to the felt emotion, is the ease with which we formulate by its means pathological cases and normal cases under a common scheme. In every asylum we find examples of absolutely unmotived fear, anger, melancholy, or conceit; and others of an equally unmotived apathy which persists in spite of the best of outward reasons why it should give way. In the former cases we must suppose the nervous machinery to be so "labile" in some one emotional direction, that almost every stimulus, however inappropriate, will cause it to upset in that way, and as a consequence to engender the particular complex of feelings of which the psychic body of the emotion consists. Thus, to take one special instance, if inability to draw deep breath, fluttering of the heart, and that peculiar epigastric change felt as "precordial anxiety," with an irresistible tendency to take a somewhat crouching attitude and to sit still, and with perhaps other visceral processes not now known, all spontaneously occur together in a certain person; his feeling of their combination *is* the emotion of dread, and he is the victim of what is known as morbid fear. A friend who has had occasional attacks of this most distressing of all maladies, tells me

[3] This is the opposite of what happens in injuries to the brain, whether from outward violence, inward rupture or tumor, or mere starvation from disease. The cortical permeability seems reduced, so that excitement, instead of propagating itself laterally through the ideational channels as before tends to take the downward track into the organs of the body. The consequence is that we have tears, laughter, and temper-fits, on the most insignificant provocation, accompanying a proportional feebleness in logical thought and the power of volitional attention and decision.

that in his case the whole drama seems to centre about the region of the heart and respiratory apparatus, that his main effort during the attacks is to get control of his inspirations and to slow his heart, and that the moment he attains to breathing deeply and to holding himself erect, the dread, *ipso facto*, seems to depart.[4]

The account given to Brachet by one of his own patients of her opposite condition, that of emotional insensibility, has been often quoted, and deserves to be quoted again:

> I still continue (she says) to suffer constantly; I have not a moment of comfort, and no human sensations. Surrounded by all that can render life happy and agreeable, still to me the faculty of enjoyment and of feeling is wanting—both have become physical impossibilities. In everything, even in the most tender caresses of my children, I find only bitterness. I cover them with kisses, but there is something between their lips and mine; and this horrid something is between me and all the enjoyments of life. My existence is incomplete. The functions and acts of ordinary life, it is true, still remain to me; but in every one of them there is something wanting—to wit, the feeling which is proper to them, and the pleasure which follows them. . . . . *Each of my senses, each part of my proper self, is as if it were separated from me and can no longer afford me any feeling; this impossibility seems to depend upon a void which I feel in the front of my head, and to be due to the diminution of the sensibility over the whole surface of my body, for it seems to me that I never actually reach the objects which I touch.* . . . . *I feel well enough the changes of temperature on my skin* but *I no longer experience the internal feeling of the air when I breathe.*

---

[4] It must be confessed that there are cases of morbid fear in which objectively the heart is not much perturbed. These however fail to prove anything against our theory, for it is of course possible that the cortical centres normally percipient of dread as a complex of cardiac and other organic sensations due to real bodily change, should become *primarily* excited in brain-disease, and give rise to an hallucination of the changes being there,—an hallucination of dread, consequently, coexistent with a comparatively calm pulse, &c. I say it is possible, for I am ignorant of observations which might test the fact. Trance, ecstasy, &c., offer analogous examples—not to speak of ordinary dreaming. Under all these conditions one may have the liveliest subjective feelings, either of eye or ear, or of the more visceral and emotional sort, as a result of pure nerve-central activity, with complete peripheral repose. Whether the subjective strength of the feeling be due in these cases to the actual energy of the central disturbance, or merely to the narrowing of the field of consciousness, need not concern us. In the asylum cases of melancholy, there is usually a narrowing of the field.

. . . . All this would be a small matter enough, but for its frightful result, which is that of the impossibility of any other kind of feeling and of any sort of enjoyment, although I experience a need and desire of them that render my life an incomprehensible torture. Every function, every action of my life remains, but deprived of the feeling that belongs to it, of the enjoyment that should follow it. My feet are cold, I warm them, but gain no pleasure from the warmth. I recognize the taste of all I eat, without getting any pleasure from it. . . . . My children are growing handsome and healthy, everyone tells me so, I see it myself, but the delight, the inward comfort I ought to feel, I fail to get. Music has lost all charm for me, I used to love it dearly. My daughter plays very well, but for me it is mere noise. That lively interest which a year ago made me hear a delicious concert in the smallest air their fingers played,—that thrill, that general vibration which made me shed such tender tears,—all that exists no more.[5]

Other victims describe themselves as closed in walls of ice or covered with an india-rubber integument, through which no impression penetrates to the sealed-up sensibility.

If our hypothesis be true, it makes us realize more deeply than ever how much our mental life is knit up with our corporeal frame, in the strictest sense of the term. Rapture, love, ambition, indignation, and pride, considered as feelings, are fruits of the same soil with the grossest bodily sensations of pleasure and of pain. But it was said at the outset that this would be affirmed only of what we then agreed to call the "standard" emotions; and that those inward sensibilities that appeared devoid at first sight of bodily results should be left out of our account. We had better, before closing, say a word or two about these latter feelings.

They are, the reader will remember, the moral, intellectual, and aesthetic feelings. Concords of sounds, of colours, of lines, logical consistencies, teleological fitnesses, affect us with a pleasure that seems ingrained in the very form of the representation itself, and to borrow nothing from any reverberation surging up from the parts below the brain. The Herbartian psychologists have tried to distinguish feelings due to the *form* in which ideas may be arranged. A geometrical demonstration may be as "pretty" and an act of justice as "neat" as a drawing or a tune, although the prettiness and neatness seem here to be a pure matter of sensation,

[5] Quoted by Semal: *De la Sensibilité générale dans les Affections mélancoliques*, Paris, 1876, pp. 130–135.

and there to have nothing to do with sensation. We have, then, or some of us seem to have, genuinely *cerebral* forms of pleasure and displeasure, apparently not agreeing in their mode of production with the so-called "standard" emotions we have been analysing. And it is certain that readers whom our reasons have hitherto failed to convince will now start up at this admission, and consider that by it we give up our whole case. Since musical perceptions, since logical ideas, can immediately arouse a form of emotional feeling, they will say: Is it not more natural to suppose that in the case if the so-called "standard" emotions, prompted by the presence of objects or the experience of events, the emotional feeling is equally immediate, and the bodily expression something that comes later and is added on?

But a sober scrutiny of the cases of pure cerebral emotion gives little force to this assimilation. Unless in them there actually be coupled with the intellectual feeling a bodily reverberation of some kind, unless we actually laugh at the neatness of the mechanical device, thrill at the justice of the act, or tingle at the perfection of the musical form, our mental condition is more allied to a judgment of *right* than to anything else. And such a judgment is rather to be classed among awarenesses of truth: it is a *cognitive* act. But as a matter of fact the intellectual feeling hardly ever does exist thus unaccompanied. The bodily sounding-board is at work, as careful introspection will show, far more than we usually suppose. Still, where long familiarity with a certain class of effects has blunted emotional sensibility thereto as much as it has sharpened the taste and judgment, we do get the intellectual emotion, if such it can be called, pure and undefiled. And the dryness of it, the paleness, the absence of all glow, as it may exist in a thoroughly expert critic's mind, not only shows us what an altogether different thing it is from the "standard" emotions we considered first, but makes us suspect that almost the entire difference lies in the fact that the bodily sounding-board, vibrating in the one case, is in the other mute. "Not so very bad" is, in a person of consummate taste, apt to be the highest limit of approving expression. "*Rien ne me choque*" is said to have been Chopin's superlative of praise of new music. A sentimental layman would feel, and ought to feel, horrified, on being admitted into such a critic's mind, to see how cold, how thin, how void of human significance, are the motives for favour or disfavour that there prevail. The capacity to make a nice spot on the wall will outweigh a picture's whole content; a foolish trick of words will preserve a poem; an utterly meaningless fitness of sequence in one musical composition set at naught any amount of "expressiveness" in another.

I remember seeing an English couple sit for more than an hour on a piercing February day in the Academy at Venice before the celebrated "Assumption" by Titian; and when I, after being chased from room to room by the cold, concluded to get into the sunshine as fast as possible and let the pictures go, but before leaving drew reverently near to them to learn with what superior forms of susceptibility they might be endowed, all I overheard was the woman's voice murmuring: "What a *deprecatory* expression her face wears! What self-abne*gation!* How *unworthy* she feels of the honour she is receiving!" Their honest hearts had been kept warm all the time by a glow of spurious sentiment that would have fairly made old Titian sick. Mr. Ruskin somewhere makes the (for him) terrible admission that religious people as a rule care little for pictures, and that when they do care for them they generally prefer the worst ones to the best. Yes! in every art, in every science, there is the keen perception of certain relations being *right* or not, and there is the emotional flush and thrill consequent thereupon. And these are two things, not one. In the former of them it is that experts and masters are at home. The latter accompaniments are bodily commotions that they may hardly feel, but that may be experienced in their fulness by *crétins* and Philistines in whom the critical judgment is at its lowest ebb. The "marvels" of Science, about which so much edifying popular literature is written, are apt to be "caviare" to the men in the laboratories. Cognition and emotion are parted even in this last retreat,—who shall say that their antagonism may not just be one phase of the world-old struggle known as that between the spirit and the flesh?—a struggle in which it seems pretty certain that neither party will definitively drive the other off the field.

To return now to our starting-point, the physiology of the brain. If we suppose its cortex to contain centres for the perception of changes in each special sense-organ, in each portion of the skin, in each muscle, each joint, and each viscus, and to contain absolutely nothing else, we still have a scheme perfectly capable of representing the process of the emotions. An object falls on a sense-organ and is apperceived by the appropriate cortical centre; or else the latter, excited in some other way, gives rise to an idea of the same object. Quick as a flash, the reflex currents pass down through their preordained channels, alter the condition of muscle, skin and viscus; and these alterations, apperceived like the original object, in as many specific portions of the cortex, combine with it in consciousness and transform it from an object-simply-apprehended into an object-emotionally-felt. No new principles have to be invoked, nothing is postulated beyond the ordinary reflex circuit, and the topical centres admitted in one shape or another by all to exist.

It must be confessed that a crucial test of the truth of the hypothesis is quite as hard to obtain as its decisive refutation. A case of complete internal and external corporeal anaesthesia, without motor alteration or alteration of intelligence except emotional apathy, would afford, if not a crucial test, at least a strong presumption, in favour of the truth of the view we have set forth; whilst the persistence of strong emotional feeling in such a case would completely overthrow our case. Hysterical anaesthesias seem never to be complete enough to cover the ground. Complete anaesthesias from organic disease, on the other hand, are excessively rare. In the famous case of Remigius Leims, no mention is made by the reporters of his emotional condition, a circumstance which by itself affords no presumption that it was normal, since as a rule nothing ever *is* noticed without a pre-existing question in the mind. Dr. Georg Winter has recently described a case somewhat similar,[6] and in reply to a question, kindly writes to me as follows:

The case has been for a year and a half entirely removed from my observation. But so far as I am able to state, the man was characterised by a certain mental inertia and indolence. He was tranquil, and had on the

---

[6] "Ein Fall von allgemeiner Anaesthesie," *Inaugural-Dissertation.* Heidelberg, Winter, 1882.

whole the temperament of a phlegmatic. He was not irritable, not quarrelsome, went quietly about his farm-work, and left the care of his business and house-keeping to other people. In short, he gave one the impression of a placid countryman, who has no interests beyond his work.

Dr. Winter adds that in studying the case he paid no particular attention to the man's psychic condition, as this seemed "nebensächlich" to his main purpose. I should add that the form of my question to Dr. Winter could give him no clue as to the kind of answer I expected.

Of course, this case proves nothing, but it is to be hoped that asylum-physicians and nervous specialists may begin methodically to study the relation between anæsthesia and emotional apathy. If the hypothesis here suggested is ever to be definitively confirmed or disproved it seems as if it must be by them, for they alone have the data in their hands.

P.S.—By an unpardonable forgetfulness at the time of despatching my MS. to the Editor, I ignored the existence of the extraordinary case of total anaesthesia published by Professor Strümpell in *Ziemssen's Deutsches Archiv für klinische Medicin* xxii., 321, of which I had nevertheless read reports at the time of its publication. (*Cf.* first report of the case in *Mind* X., 263, translated from *Pflüger's Archiv.*—ED.) I believe that it constitutes the only remaining case of the sort in medical literature, so that with it our survey is complete. On referring to the original, which is important in many connections, I found that the patient, a shoemaker's apprentice of 15, entirely anaesthetic, inside and out, with the exception of one eye and one ear, had shown *shame* on the occasion of soiling his bed, and *grief*, when a formerly favourite dish was set before him, at the thought that he could no longer taste its flavour. As Dr. Strümpell seemed however to have paid no special attention to his psychic states, so far as these are matter for our theory, I wrote to him in a few words what the essence of the theory was, and asked him to say whether he felt sure the grief and shame mentioned were real feelings in the boy's mind, or only the reflex manifestations provoked by certain perceptions, manifestations that an outside observer might note, but to which the boy himself might be insensible.

Dr. Strümpell has sent me a very obliging reply, of which I translate the most important passage.

"I must indeed confess that I naturally failed to institute with my *Anaesthetiker* observations as special as the sense of your theory would require. Nevertheless I think I can decidedly make the statement, that he was by no means completely lacking in emotional affections. In addition to the feelings of *grief* and *shame* mentioned in my paper, I recall distinctly that he showed, *e.g.*, *anger*, and frequently quarrelled with the hospital attendants. He also manifested *fear* lest I should punish him. In short, I do not think that my case speaks exactly in favour of your theory. On the other hand, I will not affirm that it positively refutes your theory. For my case was certainly one of a very centrally conditioned anaesthesia (perception-anaesthesia, like that of hysterics) and therefore the conduction of outward impressions may in him have been undisturbed."

I confess that I do not see the relevancy of the last consideration, and this makes me suspect that my own letter was too briefly or obscurely expressed to put my correspondent fully in possession of my own thought. For his reply still makes no explicit reference to anything but the outward manifestations of emotion in the boy. Is it not at least conceivable that, just as a stranger, brought into the boy's presence for the first time, and seeing him eat and drink and satisfy other natural necessities, would suppose him to have the feelings of hunger, thirst, &c., until informed by the boy himself that he did all these things with no feeling at all but that of sight and sound—is it not, I say, at least possible, that Dr. Strümpell, addressing no direct introspective questions to his patient, and the patient not being of a class from which one could expect voluntary revelations of that sort, should have similarly omitted to discriminate between a feeling and its habitual motor accompaniment, and erroneously taken the latter as proof that the former was there? Such a mistake is of course possible, and I must therefore repeat Dr. Strümpell's own words, that his case does not yet refute my theory. Should a similar case recur, it ought to be interrogated as to the inward emotional state that co-existed with the outward expressions of shame, anger, &c. And if it then turned out that the patient recognized explicitly the same mood of feeling known under those names in his former normal state, my theory would of course fall. It is, however, to me incredible that the patient should have an *identical* feeling, for the dropping out of the organic sounding-board would necessarily diminish its volume in some way. The teacher of Dr. Strümpell's patient found a mental deficiency in him during his anaesthesia, that may possibly have been due to the consequences resulting to his general intellectual vivacity from the subtraction of so important a mass of feelings, even though they were not the whole of his emotional life. Whoever wishes to extract from the next case of total anaesthesia the maximum of knowledge about the emotions, will have to interrogate the patient with some such notion as that of my article in his mind. We can define the pure psychic emotions far better by starting from such an hypothesis and modifying it in the way of restriction and subtraction, than by having no definite hypothesis at all. Thus will the publication of my article have been justified, even though the theory it advocates, rigorously taken, be erroneous. The best thing I can say for it is, that in writing it, I have almost persuaded *myself* it may be true.

THE EMOTIONS

BY

CARL GEORG LANGE, M.D.

THE EMOTIONS

A PSYCHOPHYSIOLOGICAL STUDY

CARL GEORG LANGE, M.D.

Professor of Medicine in Copenhagen

TRANSLATED BY ISTAR A. HAUPT

From the Authorized German Translation of H. Kurella, M.D.

Kant, in a passage in his *Anthropologie*, qualifies the affections as diseases of the mind.

He considers the mind normal only as long as it is under the incontrovertible and absolute control of reason. Anything that causes it to be disturbed seems to him to be abnormal and harmful to the individual.

To a more realistic school of psychology, which knows no abstract "Ideal" man, but rather "takes men as they are," such a doctrine of the soul must appear strange. It must be but a meager conception of man's existence, to consider pain and pleasure, pity and anger, defiance and humility, as conditions foreign to normal life, or even as something from which one must turn away if one wishes to recognize the actual nature of man-kind. A theory which makes the power of admiring the great, of deriving pleasure from the beautiful, and of being moved by misfortune, a disease, results in a limitation of the extent of our mental life. Such a theory will consider the imperturbable arithmetic teacher, to whom every impression is merely an impulse to draw rational conclusions, as the only normal, healthy individual. It is a strange conception of the interaction of mental powers to consider as accidental that which plays a larger and more vital part than normal reason in the mental life of most men, and which determines to a much higher degree than reason the fate of nations as well as of individuals.

Who would wish to cure an unhealthy mind, if by so doing he would rob man of all that goes to make him a sympathetic crea-

33

ture; that enables him to share the pleasure and pain of those of his kind; and to admire his like or to hate them? No,—however true it may be that we must eliminate our passions wherever it is a question of calm consideration, clear recognition, or unbiased judgment, it is undoubtedly just as true that we cannot consider an individual who can only think, recognize, judge—but not suffer, fear or rejoice—a true, healthy, complete human being, even if occasionally these abilities may be detrimental to his power of understanding and judgment.

Emotions are not only the most important factors in the life of the individual human being, but they are also the most powerful forces of nature known to us. Every page in the history of nations testifies to their invincible power.

The storm of passions has cost more lives and has destroyed more lands than hurricanes; their floods have wiped out more towns than floods of water. Wherefore, it must seem strange, indeed, to us that careful measures have not been taken to study their nature and behavior. Whereas the greatest efforts have been made to obtain knowledge of the causes and activities of other forces of nature for the sake of controlling them as much as possible, the investigation of the greatest force of all, the one which concerns us so vitally and personally, has been neglected to such an extent that we can be said scarcely to possess even the most superficial understanding of its more immediate conditions and its true nature.

In this article no attempt has been made to give a complete representation of the physiology of the emotions, or even a general review of the main points. The study is limited entirely to one aspect of the problem. It owes its origin primarily to the necessity of clearing up, for practical medical purposes of my own, the relation of the emotions to bodily conditions (often pathological); and if possible to ascertain this relation by means of a more precise, physiological method than has heretofore been attempted.

As often happens, I was led further in my work than I intended to go originally. A somewhat more searching investigation of the subject very soon led me to the conclusion that the task which I had set myself—namely, to determine (in agreement with popular

psychology) "what effects the emotions have upon body functions"—offered not only great difficulties, but in point of fact was
also absolutely impossible, simply because the question had been
put in reverse order.

It soon became apparent that to throw some light upon the
matter, the investigation must encompass a wider field because
the point of departure—namely, the conception of "Emotions"—
is entirely without scientific definiteness, especially if more rigorous
demands are made than those which would satisfy the purely
speculative psychologist.

What is an emotion? I hope the result of this little study will
be to obtain a clear, more positive conception of this term. But
even at the very outset, one meets with the necessity of setting
some sort of territorial limitation to the conception of "emotion"
for the sake of preliminary comprehension, since neither popular
nor scientific speech gives us any definition, at least, none that is
accepted generally. To say that we wish to deal here chiefly with
the "affections" does not clearly define our field of activity.

However, I do not mean to say that it would be difficult to
enumerate all the phenomena which might be included under this
heading,—all the various kinds of affections. That is of no consequence to me since I do not aim at completeness in that regard,
even if it be permissible to speak of completeness here. On the
contrary, as will be evident further on, I intend to confine myself
to a very narrow field. It is, however, of some importance to deal
with as clear a conception as possible; I mean, a conception which
includes, physiologically, only phenomena that are analagous. In
this regard, it is not possible to start from any one point that will
satisfy all conditions. Heterogeneous conceptions overlap, in
popular speech as well as in scientific psychology, because of a
certain family resemblance, so to speak. Sorrow, joy, fear, anger
and the like, on the one hand, and on the other, love, hate, scorn,
admiration, etc., are obviously two groups of phenomena which,
from the point of view of psychology, must be kept apart. I shall
retain the term "Emotions" with reference to the first group only,
whereas I shall let the others be called passions, feelings, or anything else appropriate.

Yet the line of demarcation between the two has never been clearly defined (1),[1] although it is difficult to explain why scientific psychology, at least, has not felt the necessity for a more rigorous definition. For it is absolutely necessary to keep these two apart as much as possible; at least, when one is dealing with the physiology of these phenomena (2). We cannot throw conditions such as fright, rage, joy, together with jealousy, love, desire for freedom, etc. And the difference between these two groups lies not only in the fact that the latter is more complicated, and includes dissimilar disturbances of the mind so that disturbances in imagination and reflexion especially play a part in their origin (3); but also they are complicated and heterogeneous in the conditions of their origin. Feelings such as love, hate, admiration, etc., consist of quite complex psychic phenomena, in which the emotions of joy, anger, fear, etc., enter as separate elements, the latter being simple, single phenomena.

A much greater difficulty confronts us as soon as we try to determine the scope of the individual emotions, to limit the conceptions sorrow, joy, etc., so that we may have a basis of differentiation by means of which we can consider to what affection we may attribute each emotion. This indeed seems to be the problem which presents itself as soon as an attempt is made to define the various emotions, or even to submit them to scientific investigation. What is Joy? What is Fright? The answer to such a question, at least more recently, seems to be considered entirely unnecessary, even where an exact treatment of psychology is intended (4).

On the one hand, the matter is considered obvious, as something which needs no further explanation: everyone can obtain sufficient enlightenment by drawing on his own experience. "Everybody knows what joy and sorrow are." On the other hand, the emotions are believed to be so subjective as to be outside the scope of any definition, just like the color sensation of red or blue. But as long as such a purely subjective conception is maintained, a scientific investigation of their relation is, of course, impossible.

---

[1] Numbers in parentheses refer to the author's addenda.

No object can be dealt with scientifically unless it posseses objective qualities, concerning whose properties investigators agree. By these it may become an object of general perception and understanding, and may at least be discussed. Whatever lies outside the range of discussion, as for instance color-perception or sensations of fright or anger, therefore also lies outside of the range of science. The study of colors had nothing to do with science as long as the individual knew nothing of it except the effect that colors had on him personally. The scientific color theory developed only after an objective quality of the color rays had been finally discovered by Newton. In the same way the emotions will be excluded from scientific investigation until their objective qualities are discovered and these are taken as points of departure.

It is now sufficiently well known that such processes, open to objective investigation, are present. That a man is sorry or afraid or enraged is no longer only a matter of his subjective perception, but also is easily recognized by his associates on account of various sorts of involuntary bodily manifestations, which go hand in hand with the subjective feelings of fear, joy, etc. For this reason it is difficult to conceal a strong affection. It is these physiological manifestations of emotions which serve us as stepping-stones—assuredly the only ones—to their scientific investigation. But until now, they have not been used as such. Of course, this does not mean that physiology and psychology have let these phenomena pass unnoticed. On the contrary, they were turned to with particular preference, especially in the past. Since the time of Aristotle masses of literature are on hand to explain the "Influence of the affections upon the body," or at least, the effect of particular phenomena which are included here (5).

Nevertheless, a scientific result, a clearer insight into the nature of the affections, has not yet been achieved. In spite of all these notes—for they are hardly more than notes—collected in the course of centuries, no considerable advance has been made. There are various reasons for this: in the first place, the various studies date from an early period, when the necessary physiological assumptions were almost entirely wanting. Even now, as we shall see later, they are all too meager, partly because until recently physiognomy, in its narrower sense, has been too closely adhered to. The changes of facial expression under varying emotions are precisely those manifestations which yield the least scientific results. This is partly due to the fact that they are limited to one aspect alone of the physiological manifestations, and partly to the fact that they still elude physiological analysis. Finally, and essentially, the reason lies in the fact that examinations of the affections have never been based upon these bodily manifestations, but have always considered these to be secondary phenomena, which might perhaps be interesting and important, but which, nevertheless, possessed only subordinate significance. Bodily expressions were considered to be more or less accidental concomitants of the main phenomena—the mental affection.

In fact, it might be declared without exaggeration that scientifically we have absolutely no understanding of the emotions. We have not even a shadow of insight into the nature of the affections in general, or of the individual emotions. It is thought that something is known of their mutual relation, and their similarity and dissimilarity; but this view is based solely upon indefinite impressions, and is not scientifically supported. It is said for instance that joy and sorrow are opposites. This happens to be true, as we shall see later, but it is hardly possible to say that we understand fully wherein this opposition lies, or even that we can form a clear idea of it. To cite another case: anger is probably often considered to stand in closer relation to sorrow than to joy,[2] whereas physiological investigation will prove that the opposite is actually the case, etc., etc.

If now, although no scientific definition of the affections can be given at the outset, I proceed, in this investigation from the traditional conceptions and the popular affections, and put the question in the following way: "What bodily manifestations accompany each of the affections?" I do so with full consciousness of the fact that the problem is hereby reversed, and that the starting point is anything but precise and scientific. Nevertheless, this way will presumably prove to be the most expedient one for reaching a tentative conception. This method does not differ too much from

[2] Cf. Kant's definition of anger as a fright which suddenly awakens the power of resistance to threatened evil (*Anthropologie*, Bk. 3, §73). Even though anger and fright are diametrically opposed physiologically.

the popular one, and it is possible by means of it to reach the correct conclusion, even if in a more round-about way. The investigation will be limited to only a few of the most decided and best defined affections: joy, sorrow, fear, anger, and to a certain extent, embarrassment, suspense, and disappointment. The reason for this limitation is that I am interested in the demonstrations of the method of scientific analysis of emotions rather than in carrying it out in full detail, and that in the case of most of the other emotions, the bodily manifestations are so slight that they cannot be used in any of the present crude and insufficient methods for physiological analysis.

Material and methods are unfortunately more limited in the physiological investigation of the affections than in any other physiological investigation. The most important method, the experimental, is here of but little, if of any use, since animal psychology is still too vague to draw conclusions from the study of animals as to the behavior of human beings. It is also only rarely that opportunities present themselves for even approximately accurate experimental work with human beings. And so we are reduced essentially to simple observation of ourselves and others, to "clinical" observation, to use the medical term, where all observation of the symptoms which appear casually are included, as opposed to experimental investigation, where the symptoms are controlled. Especially instructive are the cases where the affections appear with such powerful and persistent disturbances that we enter into the field of pathology. The degree of intensity which the symptoms reach here, and especially the fact that, owing to their seriousness, they fall under the observation and treatment of competent physicians, makes the study of the "emotional" diseases particularly important for psychology, or, rather, it will be made so as soon as they are dealt with more systematically.

We must compare these conscious observations with the simpler, less voluntary experiences that generations have recorded in the past, and which have become the property of popular consciousness. These are preserved in many various verbal expressions and figures of speech. For these, we turn gladly to the poet. In articles on the bodily expression of the emotions, we usually find innumerable quotations from earlier and more recent poets. This fact may be justified in so far as a picturesque or striking expression of the external characteristics of emotions is often found in poetical works. But we must not look there for new material for observation. Poets are no longer "*doctores huius scientiae praecipui*"[3] as at the time of Bacon, for the problems of our time lead us elsewhere than to the "innumerable" subtle questions with which former representatives of this branch of psychology dealt.

New-born infants offer very interesting material for observation along certain lines, particularly because of the relative simplicity of the conditions and the predominance of affections undisturbed and uninterfered with by reason; also because of the feedom from acquired conventional expression of the affections.

This condition holds also for the study of the affections among primitive peoples, where the emotions are often very strongly and immediately expressed. On the other hand, we meet with the same difficulties in dealing with infants and primitive peoples, as we do when we study animal behavior, namely the uncertainty of our psychological understanding, the inevitable consequence of the subject's unsatisfactory reports.

SORROW

The most striking characteristic in the physiology and also in the physiognomy of sorrow is its inhibitory effect upon the voluntary motor apparatus. The paralysis caused by sorrow is, however, not nearly as pronounced as that produced by fright. As we shall see later, in the case of sorrow, the motor weakening seldom goes further than to require effort and exertion for the performance of movements which ordinarily are accomplished with ease. There is, in other words, a feeling of lassitude, and, as in the case of any fatigue, the movements are effected but slowly, and languidly, with effort, want of power and pleasure, and are therefore reduced to a minimum. This also accounts for the external expression by which a sorrowful person is so easily recognized. He walks slowly, uncertainly, dragging his steps and letting his arms hang limp at his sides. His voice is weak and

[3]*De dignitate et augmentis scienitarum*, lib. 7, cap. 3.

thin, as a result of the weakened activity of the expiratory and laryngeal muscles. He prefers to sit silent and lost in thought. The "latent innervation" (6) of the muscles also is conspicuously weakened. His neck is bent, his head droops—"cast down," "bent" by woe,—his face is lengthened and narrowed by the laxity of the muscles of the cheek and jaw; his jaw may even hang down. His eyes appear large, as is always the case when the *orbicularis oculi* muscles are weakened. On the other hand, they may be abnormally covered by the upper lid, as happens when the *levator palpebrae superioris* muscles become weakened. Concomitant with this weakened condition of the voluntary nerve and muscle apparatus of the entire body, there appears also a feeling of lassitude, of heaviness, as if you were weighed down by something. You feel "oppressed," "dejected," you speak of "weighty" sorrow, you must bear your woe, whereas you must bridle your anger or joy. Many are so overpowered by sorrow that they can not even hold themselves erect. The sufferer leans on or supports himself by the surroundings, falls on his knees, or in desperation even throws himself upon the floor, as Romeo did in the monk's cell.

This weakness of the whole apparatus of nerves and muscles of animal life, and subordination to the will, is, however, only one aspect of the physiology of sorrow. Another aspect, hardly less important, and perhaps even more significant in its consequences, belongs to another division of the motor mechanism; to the involuntary, organic muscles, especially to those which are found in the walls of the blood-vessels, and by whose constriction these vessels may be narrowed. The vascular muscles and their nerves, together with the vaso-motor apparatus, function in exactly the opposite way from that in which the voluntary muscular apparatus functions. Whereas the former became flaccid and weakened, on the contrary, the vascular muscles contract more than usually, so that the blood is forced out of the capillaries and decreases the supply to the tissues, and organs of the body (7). The immediate consequences of insufficient blood-supply are pallor, collapse and hypoemia. The pale color and sunken features are just those peculiarities which, together with the weakened face muscles, produce the lineaments characteristic of the woeful, and give the impression of such rapid emaciation that it cannot possibly be attributed to either a change in metabolism or to uncompensated consumption of the body tissues. Other regular results of insufficient blood supply to the skin are sensations of cold, cold shivers, difficulty in warming the body and sensitiveness to cold. These conditions belong also to the rather constant attributes of sorrow. The bloodless condition of the skin is no doubt paralleled in the condition of the internal organs, and though not so obvious, it may be recognized, nevertheless, by various symptoms. This supposition is supported by the fact of the decreased secretions, at least of those which are controlled more easily. The mouth becomes dry, the tongue clings to the palate, and a bitter taste is produced, which seems to be a simple consequence of the drying of the tongue.[4] In the case of nursing women, the secretion of milk is decreased or often ceases entirely. As a contrast to the above mentioned physiological symptoms, there is one of the most regular attributes of sorrow which is weeping, with the plentiful tear secretion and the swollen, reddened condition of the face, the increased flow of the mucous secretion of the nose: all appearances which point to a considerable dilation of the skin tissues of the face and of the mucous membrane. And yet it may very well be assumed that such a dilation follows as a reaction to a previous constriction, that is, of a relaxing of the vascular muscles after their extreme tension. Similarly, we frequently find fatigue or laxity as results of any overstraining of the nerves and muscles. This, for example, may be strikingly manifested whenever a part of the skin which has been exposed to intense cold is suddenly brought to conditions of normal temperature (8). This explanation of weeping seems to become more plausible when we consider the fact that weeping does not begin until the sorrow has abated somewhat. This circumstance is popularly understood to mean that "Tears bring relief," and we say "Cry it out," especially since at the same time solace is found in weeping.

If the capillaries of the lungs constrict suddenly so that these

---

[4] The expression "bitter woe" is commonly considered to be metaphorical, but it may well be assumed that it originated from the often very intense bitter taste that accompanies the perception of depressing impressions.

organs are deprived of their normal blood supply, then a feeling of suffocation arises, just as always happens when the respiratory mechanism suffers. We also feel a pressure on the chest (oppression) and these "torturing, depressing" sensations add to the sufferings of the sorrowful who try involuntarily to relieve themselves by deep, slow breathing—sighs—a method which anyone who experiences difficulty in breathing from any cause whatever, instinctively pursues.

The deficient blood-supply to the brain is manifested by mental lassitude, dullness, a feeling of mental fatigue and effort, by an indisposition for mental work and frequently by sleeplessness.[5] In the same way, as we shall see later, it is probably the absence of blood in the motor organs of the brain which is the fundamental cause of the weakened force of the voluntary movements.

If the anxiety be lasting so that the above mentioned disturbances of the blood-supply continue for a year and a day, then external changes in the organs must occur, as always happens if the blood supply and consequently the nourishment be insufficient for any length of time. These changes are well known in pathology, under the name of "atrophies," but as yet too little attention has been paid to the possible effects of prolonged emotional disturbances, and modern pathology is all too ready to laugh at old beliefs in the fundamental significance of certain organic affections. Nevertheless, there can be little doubt, however difficult or impossible it may be to furnish positive proof, that continuous sorrow may have an atrophying effect upon the internal organs, especially since the effects upon the visible parts of the body are so conspicuous. It is well known that a sorrowful person ages prematurely, but this early impression of senility depends solely upon atrophied changes in the skin and other external parts of the body. The body becomes emaciated by the disappearance of all the adipose and muscular tissues. The hair turns gray because it is not sufficiently

[5] I keep for another occasion the proof that sleeplessness is caused by the spasmodic contraction of the brain cells. The much controverted physiological explanation of sleep may be supposed to be that sleep is caused by a periodic laxity of the brain cells, by a loss of tone resulting from fatigue of the nerves of the brain.

nourished and because the pigment vanishes and is prematurely lost (9). Similarly the wrinkling of the skin and the furrowing of the brow by sorrow,—both simple phenomena of atrophy,— occur prematurely and contribute to the early ageing of the sufferer. In short, all atrophic changes in the visible parts of the body that take place with the normal ageing are hastened by sorrow. Is there then anything improbable in the assumption that changes analogous to the senile changes take place in the case of the internal organs?[6]

The bodily phenomena which accompany sorrow may also be explained on the basis of paralysis of the voluntary muscles, and a kind of convulsive condition of the vascular muscles.

JOY

In popular consciousness, joy constitutes the opposite of sorrow, and an examination of its physiological manifestations agrees with this direct conception. The "Effect of Joy upon the Body"— to use this popular mode of expressing the relation—is in fact the opposite of that of sorrow. In the case of joy, a heightening of the functioning of the voluntary motor apparatus takes place, together with a dilation of the arterioles and capillaries. These are the two fundamental physiological symptoms by which the joyous one sustains his entire peculiar physiology. The heightened function of the voluntary muscles and nerves causes the feeling of lightness of joy, such as everyone experiences whose muscles are strong and unfatigued.[7] He feels an increased motor impulse, moves swiftly and alertly, and gesticulates violently. Children jump, dance, clap their hands for joy. The facial muscles contract as a result of heightened latent innervation, and become round compared with the long, lax, hanging features of the melancholic person. Smiling and laughing are the results of the heightened impulse of facial and breathing muscles, as are also the high-pitched voice,

[6] A well-known English pathologist has given proof in a series of cases that emotional complaints may lead to atrophy of the kidneys. (Dr. Clifford Allbut, *British Medical Journal*, 10 February, 1877.)

[7] To explain this feeling of lightness a positive decrease in body weight was formerly assumed. Cf. de Marées, *De animi perturbatione in corpora potentia*. 1775 (Ludwig, *Scriptores neurolog. minores*, Tome IV).

singing, rejoicing and the expression of involuntary impulses of the laryngeal and respiratory muscles. The eyes of a joyous person beam, sparkle, in short, assume a peculiar playful expression, which is due to the combined contraction of the lid-muscles (*orbicularis oculi palpebrarum* and *levator palpebrae*), to be seen in connection with the pupilary change.[8] The general dilation of the capillaries in joy results very strikingly in an increased flow of blood to the skin. A child's or a young girl's skin, which is white and transparent, reddens and glows with pleasure. The joyous person feels warm, his skin becomes fuller, he swells with pleasure. Increased glandular secretion also is observed: it is a common expression of satisfaction to say "the mouth waters" and "tears come easy."

Whereas the woe-begone person with his slow movements, his bent figure, his sunken features, assumes the appearance of an old man, contrariwise the joyous man appears youthful because of his swift and powerful movements, his singing and loud speaking —"Joy rejuvenates." But it is not only the external stamp of health which accompanies joy. Whereas in the case of sorrow the body-organs become aged because of the lack of nourishment due to the constricted state of the blood-vessels, normal circulation produces just the opposite effect in a contented person. A rich blood supply to the organs and tissues of the body is naturally conducive to a strong nourishing activity, and hence all parts of the body thrive and are long preserved. The contented, active person is well-nourished and keeps young. That fat men are jovial—or rather, that jovial men are fat—is commonly accepted. It is based upon sound fact, that despots like to be surrounded by fat men,[9] since their thriving condition bears witness of their contentedness, and therefore they are not easily dangerous. The part which the brain plays in the increased flow of the blood, as probably all parts of the body share it in a joyful mood, leads us to make the supposition that mental functions take place rapidly;

[8] It seems to me that the pupil contracts in joy, which would pre-suppose heightened innervation of the superior division of the *oculomotorius*. Wilks, on the other hand, believes that the pupil dilates, but he records no observations. (Bain, April, 1883, p. 4.)

[9] Shakespeare, *Julius Caesar*, Act I., Sc. 2.

there is a flow of ideas and fancies. A joyous person talks rapidly and fluently; his work proceeds swiftly, not only because his muscles are strong, but also because he reaches decisions quickly and puts them into prompt execution.

FRIGHT

Fright is, as has been indicated above, closely related to sorrow. We find the same paralyzing effect on the voluntary motor apparatus, the same convulsive conditions of the constrictor muscles, only we find both appearing more suddenly and in a more exaggerated degree. To this, however, we must add another condition which we did not observe in the case of sorrow, namely, a similar convulsive contraction of other organic muscles. In sorrow this is limited to the vascular muscles. The essential physiological difference between sorrow and fright lies in the fact that in the latter, the convulsive spasmodic condition of the voluntary muscles is shared by all muscles as far as can be judged, whereas in the former it is limited to individual groups of muscles. How conspicuous it is that the paralyzation due to fright is stronger than that due to sorrow is evident from the common verbal expression for the two phenomena. A man is "burdened with," "weighed down by," "bent with" sorrow, but he is "paralyzed" with fear, is motionless, petrified, transfixed by fright. The paralysis of the muscles of speech makes it difficult or impossible to utter a word; the voice becomes hoarse and broken; he is "struck dumb" with terror. The tongue becomes immovable, the face relaxes, the eyes are very large, motionless, staring, fixed, because of the paralysis of the muscles of the lid. A person overcome by a sudden fear may fall down paralyzed, or the innervation of the muscles may at least be so uncertain as to make him quake, tremble, stammer with fear.

It is characteristic in the case of fright as contrasted with sorrow that the paralysis of the voluntary muscles is often preceded by a momentary convulsive twitch in which a sudden start is manifested, and there is a cry in the first instant of fear. That depends upon the suddenness of the effect, which leads to the paralysis, and it has several pathological analogues. If a motor nerve is suddenly crushed, the corresponding muscles are momentarily contracted before paralysis sets in; but if the nerve be slowly and gradually pressed, then the paralysis takes place equally and gradually with no preliminary contractions. The convulsive contraction of the constrictor muscles because of fright and the resulting lack of blood in the skin occasions here and there, only more suddenly and to a higher degree, pallor,[10] coldness, a "cold shiver," (the blood "freezes"), and numbness. It is probably this sudden and complete lack of blood in the skin which causes the very rapid turning gray of the hair, as is sometimes observed to be the result of extreme terror. Reliable examples of the sudden "falling out" of the hair have been found due to fright (10).[11] In spite of the lack of blood in the skin, it may be covered with sweat, but with a "cold sweat." There is no explanation for this; however, I may mention that according to the more recent investigations of sweat secretion, there is no discrepancy between the increased secretion and the decreased blood supply to the skin. It is not exactly known in what relation other secretions stand to fright, but on the whole they decrease or even cease entirely. So, for example, in the case of the salivary secretions: the mouth becomes dry, the tongue clings to the roof of the mouth. It is a well-known fact that the secretion of milk in the case of nursing women decreases, and that existing menstruation may cease as the result of fright. Vascular convulsions and consequent deficiency in the blood supply always lead to shivers, trembling, chattering teeth, whatever their cause may be. They are well-known in fever or as the sudden effects of cold on the skin, and these too belong to the characteristic manifestations of fear. "Shiver," "shudder," "tremble" are, in fact synonymous expressions for a "sensation of fear" and for the "power to inspire fear." Comparisons between the sensations of fear, cold or fever are met with frequently in verbal expressions or in popular consciousness.[12] At first, fear acts upon the heart in such a way as to cause an

[10] "Go prick thy face and over-red thy fear, thou lily-liver'd boy." *Macbeth*, Act V., Sc. 3.

[11] Older pathologists have assumed that the blood actually coagulated under the influence of fear. *Sanguis in toto coagulatur.* (Willis, *De anima brutorum*, Cap. 9.)

[12] Cf. The Danish *"Buxefeber;"* fever-terror, the cold hand of fear, etc.

increased activity; but overwhelming fright seems to paralyze the heart and thus even cause death (11).

Whereas fright, if we were to confine ourselves to the above mentioned attributes, might be looked upon as a more intense or acute form of sorrow, there is, as has been pointed out, a large class of phenomena, by means of which we may recognize that fear has its own peculiar physiognomy, which is very different from that of sorrow. They are those symptoms which are caused by the apparent participation in the general convulsive condition of all the voluntary organic muscles, that are under no control of the will, causing movements and contractions of our inner organs, whereas in sorrow, the participation is limited to the vascular muscles. In the discussion on the convulsion of the vascular muscles, I have already mentioned the effect of fright upon the heart action. Perhaps these disturbances which aid considerably in distinguishing fright from sorrow should be assigned to that department. Rembrandt, as is well known, did not hesitate to depict realistically the effect of the convulsive contraction of the bladder of the unfortunate Ganymede, who found himself suddenly hovering between heaven and earth, his life depending upon the grasp of the eagle and the durability of his shirt.

That young recruits, on the eve of battle, are often confronted with the necessity of stepping out of rank, and are not always the pleasantest neighbors as long as they remain in rank, is due to the uncontrollable effect of fear upon the muscles of the intestines (12). It is apparent to any one who has suffered from fear, that every strong and convulsive peristaltic motion may very well be accompanied by colic pains: "cramps." The phenomena considered here belong to the more drastic concomitants of fear, which indeed usually occur only in the case of youthful individuals and members of the lower classes,—in short of those who offer favorable conditions for violent emotional phenomena (see below). There is another group of phenomena which depend upon the same physiological influence on the system of involuntary muscles, and it is by means of these that fright assumes its peculiar pathetic physiognomy when we speak of the hair "standing on end," with terror. This expression, even though somewhat exaggerated, applies to the effect of the spasmodic contraction of the fine muscle-fibers attached to the hair bulbs in the skin; "goose-flesh" is due to the same cause. The "protruding" eyes which "bulge" from their sockets and the enlarged pupils point to an irritation of the sympathetic nervous system, just as the vascular spasm does.

In the case of many individuals sudden fright arouses a peculiar subjective sensation, a sticking or pricking, which often spreads from the abdomen upwards, and is particularly noticeable on the tongue, and frequently extends over the entire body, even to the tips of the fingers and toes. To this sensation a feeling of oppression is often added, a torturing, constricting sensation, especially in the throat—"choking." The first mentioned of these sensations is undoubtably an eccentric one (projected) (13), and arises through stimulation of the cerebral organs of sensation, conditioned by the sudden contraction of the blood vessels. They have the character of subjective sensations arising in the brain, and nothing is more common than such sensations in cases of functional or organic diseases of the brain. The origin of the sensations of suffocation which so often accompany fright is less obvious. According to their form there is nothing to stand in the way of considering them eccentric perceptions which come from the spinal cord; a stimulation of the gray matter of the cord, brought about by the spasmodic contraction of its fine arteries, can undoubtably have such sensations as a consequence, but they are not as characteristic as the corresponding brain symptoms and therefore not as conclusive. Of all emotional disturbances, fright is probably the one which most frequently causes symptoms and conditions of disease that are often lasting and even incurable. It is not my purpose here to enter into the entire pathological meaning of the affections. I wish only to remark briefly that, even with the most critical estimation of the facts, it is quite indubitable that fright may cause paralysis, epilepsy, mental disturbance, and numerous other nervous diseases, and similarly, as I have already stated, sudden fright may lead even to death.

ANGER—RAGE

As a rule, it is undoubtedly easy for an observer to distinguish an embittered, raging person, from a cheerful, joyous one, by general bodily conditions, appearance, and attitude. But if the physiological conditions characteristic of these two affections are analyzed rather more carefully, such striking agreement of fundamental relations will be found that it is not at all easy to specify the difference.

In the first place, both anger and joy manifest a dilation of the fine blood vessels, an increased circulation to the skin, which causes reddening, heat, swelling, "turgor." An angry person "seethes," is "consumed" with anger; the blood rushes to his head he "boils," he must "cool" his wrath, work off his rage,—he swells up with rage, as is evident from these and similar figures of speech by which common popular opinions on the influence of anger upon the circulation is expressed. Yet the symptoms are on the whole more exaggerated in anger than in joy, so strong indeed that rage causes diseases and brings with it a feeling of dissatisfaction, instead of the content due to temperature increase which accompanies joy. The mucous membranes share in the increased blood supply, the eyes are bloodshot, and we find that where there is a predisposition hemorrhages may even occur; nose bleedings and lung hemorrhages have come under my personal observation.

However, the irregularities of circulation differ not alone in degree and intensity in the two cases, but in anger we find an entirely new element added of which we find no trace in joy, namely a swelling and enlargement of the great blood vessels, especially of the veins. This is most conspicuous on the forehead—"the veins of the temples swell"[13] (14), but is noticeable in other parts too—in the neck and hands for instance. In what physiological relation these phenomena stand is not perfectly clear to me: there can, of course, be no question of an actual dilation of the blood vessels as in congestion. Such a dilation is not detectable even in the larger blood vessels; nor can it be assumed that a paralysis of the insignificant muscular apparatus of these veins lies at the root of these swellings. No other explanation remains for these dilations except in the congestion of the blood resulting from some obstacle in the passage of the blood to the heart or from a defect in the secondary circuit from the right ventricle through the lungs back to the left ventricle. It is here perhaps only a question of a minor phenomenon depending upon the irregular breathing, the strong

[13] *Ora tument ira, nigrescunt sanguine venae.* Ovid, *Ars am.* III cf.

expiration in consequence of the impulse of an enraged person to call or cry out and upon all the powerful and somewhat tumultuous innervation; all of which factors favor the congestion of the blood (15). An increased innervation of the voluntary muscles and a consequent impulse to quick and forceful movements is indeed the second point in the physiology of rage. Here again we find a new agreement with joy, the physiognomy of which obtains one of its most conspicuous characteristics from the feeling of lightness, of desire for an inclination to lively movements that accompany the feeling. But this impulse is again exaggerated in anger. Instead of becoming lively, as a joyful person does, he becomes indignant—"goes up in the air," clenches his fists, waves his arms, marches with long strides ($\mu\alpha\chi\rho\alpha\beta\iota\beta\alpha s$), clenches his teeth, grits them, threatens, cries out, stamps his feet, thunders, "carries on" and yells in his rage. Whereas we can be satisfied to control our joy, we must "check" our anger like a wild animal. Even when anger, at its height ("foaming with rage"), assumes a comical aspect, when it causes its victim to jump and dance around in such a way as to remind us of a joyful individual, yet these movements are much more powerful, less controlled, clumsy, and leave us no doubt as to the actual state of affairs. The impulse of an embittered person to use his strength, the physiological, immediate expression of motor innervation; assumes a character of power and vandalism by his indiscriminate attacks upon everything that crosses his path. Unintentionally, and without discrimination, he strikes at friend and foe alike, simply to use his muscles. In some cases where there is a certain amount of self-control, he merely strikes the table with his fist, bangs the door, tears something to pieces or otherwise destroys it. He would like to demolish the earth, and he may evince a power in his rage that exceeds anything he is able to do under normal conditions. The motions of a person in a rage are, however, not distinguishable as much by their force as by their lack of control, their inaccuracy and incoördination: again the opposite state of affairs from joy. A joyful individual has easy flowing speech and a tendency to measured rhythmical movements, as in dancing. The enraged man stammers and stutters and howls when at last he is not successful in uttering a word; his muscular innervation is so uncertain that he "trembles with rage." He misses his aim—strikes blindly and consequently is little to be feared by a cold blooded opponent.

In rage—as in joy—but contrary to fear and sorrow, the face shows decided muscular contractions. Wrinkles appear upon the brow in rage, whereas, as has been mentioned above, sorrow produces folds, an effect produced by the vanishing of the skin tissue. The unequal activity of the individual facial muscles in anger and sorrow produce the difference in physiognomic expression of these two emotions. I do not want to enter into their analysis here, as has been done many times; for we lack all basis for conjecturing why it is that the facial nerves are unequally innervated in different emotions (16).

The physiological difference between pleasure and anger is, therefore, in the main, limited to a difference in the degree of dilation of the blood-vessels and the heightened innervation of the voluntary muscles, and, therefore, in the coördination (17) of the voluntary muscles. The measure of their strength ceases under the rule of anger, so that the movements become uncontrolled and inaccurate. Thus joy and anger may be considered to be the opposites of sorrow and fear and to stand in mutual relationship in the same way as the latter do. Anger also seems to have an effect upon the secretions, at least upon some, which is of the opposite nature to that produced by sorrow or fear. Where sorrow and fear cause the salivary secretion to decrease, and the tongue and larynx to become dry, we find expressions like "to foam with rage" or to "snort" that point to a very different situation in anger. In the same way, we find it a well established tradition that anger causes an increased gall secretion, "the gall runs over" in anger, he "lets his gall flow freely," for fear of letting his worry cause jaundice. Even if the observation that probably gave rise to these expressions—that a persistent, embittered disposition may cause jaundice—were true, it would be, of course, no positive proof of the increased gall secretion in any given individual. It is, in fact, difficult to designate the actual peculiar behavior of an enraged person in a physiologically incontrovertible way. It is not sufficient to say that they are mighty and uncontrolled activities. Rage is accompanied by an impulse to general violent movements, not only to satisfy the desire for simple muscular exertion, but also to gratify the craving for noisy, wanton activity which may even cause the subject pain or at least a very strong sense impression. A silent struggling with his hands and feet would not satisfy his impulse; he must hear his movements as well as feel them. He strikes the table, stamps his feet, slams the door, smashes a mirror, throws down everything that he can lay his hands on, showing a preference for hard breakable objects that make a lot of noise.[14] He might just as well exert his respiratory muscles by rapid and deep breathing, without exactly yelling and howling, but he requires "noise." In his desire for strong sense impressions, he does not spare himself bodily injury; he beats his head against the wall, tears his hair, pulls his beard, bites his lips. How can this craving for sound and sense impressions be explained physiologically? I can think of only one explanation, which has, in fact, a great deal of probability. A desire for abnormally strong sense-impressions can generally have no other cause but an abnormally weak perception of sense-impressions; a weakening of the powers of feeling, hearing, etc. It is necessary to our well-being that our central sensory nerve-cells be active to a certain degree determined by the amount of stimulation carried to them by the sensory nerves. If, for any reason whatever, as for example by a decrease in the functional power of these cells, a weakening or anaesthesia is produced, then the impulse to set these cells in their normal activity again, requires an increased external sense-impression to neutralize the decreased sensitivity. It can hardly be rigorously proved that such an anaesthesia actually exists in anger, and it is hardly legitimate to fall back upon such expressions as "blind with rage," "deafened by passion" to bear witness to the agreement of popular observation. But for the sense of feeling, the matter is quite clear. In a bitter fight, both parties may inflict upon each other serious injuries, which are not felt until the heat of the excitement has subsided. We can even beat two fighters or two dogs unmercifully, and they will take no notice.

Anger, which can present in bodily manifestations such a deceptive picture of maniacal conditions (*ira furor brevis*), becomes

[14] When Bonaparte, in Udine, wished to scare the Austrian agent by pretended rage, he did the right thing in smashing the costly china.

a cause for permanent mental disturbance as rarely as joy does, and even more rarely leads to sudden death. Galen even observed that only fright and joy kill, but not anger (περὶ αἰτιῶν συμπτο- μάτων, I. 5), and Willis (*De anima brutor*) says that women faint for joy and men die of it—but not of anger. With the restriction that death, due to joy, occurs very rarely, at least nowadays, when the affections on the whole are less overwhelming, nevertheless the rule holds generally, with the possible exception of one woman, who died at the height of her rage (*cf.* Schauen- stein, in Maschka's *Handbuch der gerichtlichen Medicin*, Vol. I, page 813) (18).

As I have mentioned before, it is not my purpose here to enter into a physiological analysis of all the bodily phenomena occurring with the different affections.

At present, I am satisfied with the attempt to deal with these four great affections and then only with their most decided forms— their conventional state—so to speak. For, indeed, it is obvious that psychic conditions exist which come under the heads of pleasure, anger, etc., but still do not fit the above representations in their physiological manifestations. This is no sign of erroneous or incomplete analysis, but merely the inevitable consequence of the circumstance that I have already discussed, namely, that the entire method of procedure used here, in which the starting point was taken from popular conceptions, is in and for itself wrong and illogical, even though it may serve as a means to attain a tentative understanding.

A complete analysis of the less strong, that is, of physically less decided affections, would hardly be successful, since our methods of observation are still so crude, and therefore I shall not attempt it here, although there are some among them whose physiological peculiarities are obvious and instructive, and I shall give them some brief discussion.

Embarrassment (shyness) is perhaps not characterized by a very decided weakening of the voluntary innervation—although a certain feeling of weakness always accompanies shyness, which gives rise to the sensation of "sinking through the floor"—yet by a very decided uncertainty of innervation, so that the amount is not properly limited and other muscles are unintentionally set in action, with excessive contraction of some and insufficient contraction of others, resulting briefly in "uncoördinated" movements.[15]

An embarrassed person has only imperfect control of his muscles. He can hardly articulate his words, stutters and stammers in speaking, gesticulates, drops whatever he is holding, rolls his eyes, walks unsteadily and even stumbles over his own feet.

A child that is very much embarrassed may present such a perfect illusion of the first symptoms of St. Vitus' dance (a disease which, in its early stages, is manifested by poor coördination of voluntary movements) as totally to deceive one. We also find a similar uncertainty of innervation of the vascular muscles. The capillaries are alternately contracted and dilated, apparently without cause, and this accounts for the rapid change of color in embarrassment, the one moment pale, and the next blushing. All these physical conditions are accompanied by a decided disturbance in the power to think, especially to concentrate on one line of thought, and the embarrassed person becomes confused, "muddled."

Suspense and expectation resemble fear in so far as they are accompanied by an apathetic condition, a tendency to contract the organic, involuntary muscles, and the various consequences of such contractions. The desire for evacuation of the different secretions and excretions; a feverish condition, which really shows some of the most striking symptoms of fever; palpitation of heart, quickened pulse, cold shivers, sleeplessness; all may be present. But the paralysis of the voluntary muscles, as in fear, is absent. On the other hand, suspense is accompanied by an animated and lively innervation of the voluntary muscular system, which expresses itself in a desire for motion. A person held in suspense becomes restless, can not stand still, but is as if on "pins" or "hot coals," "on edge." He can not sit quiet for one instant, but constantly jumps up, incessantly tramps up and down, tosses sleep-

---

[15] But of a somewhat different nature from the coördination disturbance in rage. The difference is undoubtedly due to the fact that the latter originate from functional disturbances in the brain, whereas the incoördination of embarrassment is attributable to disturbances—increased irradiation—of the functions of the spinal cord.

lessly in bed at night. We say therefore that it is "disturbing" to take part in events the results of which are unknown to us.

Disappointment is closely related to sorrow, since it is accompanied by a paralysis of the voluntary innervation, which is recognizable by a feeling of weariness, laxity ("long face") and indisposition for any effort. But all spasmodic contractions of the vessels, which are among the most conspicuous phenomena in sorrow, are absent.

The above examples will, in spite of their brevity, show sufficiently what such an analysis may lead to and what may be expected of it, with the assumptions that we can make today. They may be considered numerous and various enough to give an idea of what fundamental physiological phenomena are brought into play by our affections. It is evident that they include all functions of the nervous system, and appear partly as disturbances of innervation, i.e., as disturbances of impulses which the muscles (and also the glands) receive from the nerves; partly also, although less conspicuously, as disturbances of sensibility, as weakening or heightening of sensibility and subjective sensation; and finally, as disturbances of intelligence, by which mental life is either lowered or elevated.

The disturbances of innervation, which not only forms the most conspicuous phenomenon of the affections, but which, perhaps, as we shall try to prove later, is their real immediate physical expression, spread over the different parts of the entire system of muscles and affect now the voluntary, now the organic, and especially the vascular muscles, and the muscular apparatus of the different vital organs. The disturbances may assume various forms. The innervation may increase and the muscles contract more strongly and easily than under ordinary conditions; or the innervation may be decreased and be followed by weariness, weakness and relaxing of the blood vessels, and other muscular organs; finally, the innervation without actual increase or decrease, may reach the muscles in variable strength and produce incoördination (19) and a lack of precision in the concerted action of the muscles. The kinds of innervational disturbances of the various parts of the muscular system are not entirely analogous in different affections. One part, the voluntary muscles for instance, may be paralyzed, whereas another, the vascular muscles, may be in a convulsive condition, etc.[16]

We have, therefore, a series of different combinations which are represented by the individual affections. As we have to deal with three different systems of muscles, of which each, perhaps, may be affected in three different ways, and suffer at times only one or two functional disturbances, we seem to have 127 different combinations to give somatic forms of affections, and this only with regard to disturbances of innervation. Of course, we can not assume *a priori* that all these hypothetical combinations actually exist, while on the other hand the variabilities of the relative strength of the phenomena require an endless number of steps. We could represent the seven above mentioned forms of affections by the following scheme.

Weakness of voluntary innervation.

Weakness of voluntary innervation + vascular contraction = disappointment.

Weakness of voluntary innervation + vascular contraction + convulsion of organic muscles = fright.

Weakness of voluntary innervation + incoördination = embarrassment.

Increase of voluntary innervation + spasm of voluntary muscles = suspense.

Increase of voluntary innervation + vascular dilation = joy.

Increase of voluntary innervation + vascular dilation and incoördination = anger.

It is clear that it is not correct to state offhand as a general rule of affections, that they are accompanied by increased muscular activity,[17] and the division of the affections into active and passive, sthenic or asthenic, or however this contrast is to be expressed, is unjustified, both from the physiological and the psychological

[16] Perhaps, however, the functional disturbance of the vascular and other organic muscles is always the same.

[17] The diffuse discharge, which accompanies feelings of every sort, produces an effect on the body, namely, stimulating the musculature. These feelings arouse bodily activity, which is the more lively, the more intense the feelings are. The most striking peculiarity of the discharge, which accompanies feelings of every sort, is the circumstance that it arouses muscular contraction, which is proportional to the degree of feeling. (H. Spencer, *Principles of Psychology*, II, §§496, 497.)

point of view, as we shall endeavor to show. Most emotions possess an active as well as a passive, a sthenic and an asthenic element, and some possess even a third, which we cannot call either active or passive.

And so, a question arises concerning the various physical phenomena of the affections, whose answer is of considerable significance for the physiology of the affections, namely, whether these phenomena are physiologically of equal value, are parallel; or whether certain appearances are to be considered as caused by others, and secondary to these; whether, for example, paralysis and vascular convulsions of a mournful person are due immediately to one and the same cause, or whether the original influence acted only on one of these manifestations and that this one then caused the others. In this last case, the further question arises: Which is primary, and which is secondary?

Now, all the phenomena discussed so far can be reduced to two main groups: changes in the vascular innervation and changes in the functions of the other nerves—and since, according to all our physiological experiences, we can not assume that disturbances of functions of the second group may become vasomotor changes, whereas there is no *a priori* objection to the opposite state of affairs, the problem finally reduces to the following question: Is it possible that vasomotor disturbances, varied dilation of the blood vessels, and consequent excess of blood, in the separate organs, are the real, primary effects of the affections, whereas the other phenomena,—motor abnormalities, sensation paralysis, subjective sensations, disturbances of secretion and intelligence—are only secondary disturbances, which have their cause in anomalies of vascular innervation? Is it not, for example, possible that the muscular weakness in the case of an anxious person may be due to the fact that his nervous system may receive too little blood just as his skin and other organs do, due to the contraction of the fine arteries; and that the power and wildness of rage may be due to the excessive blood supply to the brain, as this organ surely must be involved, just as much as the skin and mucous membrane?

Our insight into the physiology of the nervous system is still incomplete, especially our understanding of the very important questions of the significance of the blood contained in the nervous organs in relation to their functions. In the face of this incomplete comprehension of the subject, it is obvious that the question as stated here cannot be answered with any decisiveness. Nevertheless, this much is known positively, that the individual parts of the nervous system; brain, spinal cord, etc.; are greatly influenced in their functional power by the condition of their blood supply. An excessive blood supply, as well as a deficient one, is a symptom of disease. We can easily convince ourselves of the significance of excessive blood supply to the head by a very simple experiment on ourselves; if we press the large pulse-arteries in the neck, we rob the brain of its normal blood supply, and the immediate results of this disturbance are dizziness, sensations of weakness, and faintness, decreased consciousness, which soon forces us to terminate the experiment, whereupon the conditions immediately become normal again. But if we interrupt the circulation by means of a bandage, as is sometimes done in surgery, there results a paralysis of that side of the body which is controlled by the motor impulses of that side of the brain in question. This paralysis endures until the circulation reaches a state of equilibrium again in a round about way. Another experiment which can be performed easily on certain animals, consists in artificially cutting off the blood supply to the lower part of the spinal cord by compressing the aorta. (Stenson's experiment.) As soon as the pressure has been administered for some moments, a paralysis of the abdomen and hind legs sets in. Movement and sensation are made possible again as soon as the pressure is removed. That a human being behaves in the same way is evident in certain diseased conditions, in which the circulation through the aorta supplying most of the blood to the spinal cord is for some reason interrupted. These and similar experiments and attempts are, to be sure, crude and coarse, in comparison to the processes of vasomotor disturbances, and changes in the innervation of the fine blood-vessels, and their consequent degree of dilation. Such disturbances may show innumerable degrees and may be limited to certain parts of each organ in question, so that the effects occur in steps of intensity, and assume many forms and variations that can not be imitated experimentally. Certainly, the above facts offer sufficient proof of the immediate and far reaching effect of the varying blood-content upon the functional power of those organs which are concerned in our movements, the sensations and psychical activities. The fact that vascular spasms in the central nervous organs lie at the root of the many and often intensive disturbances of the functions of these organs, even when these are merely temporary, as for example, in epilepsy and maniacal paroxysms, is also evidence. This fact is hardly disputed by the physiologists and pathologists of today; this circumstance is certainly strongly in favor of the mutual connection between the emotions as here described.

If, then, no essential objection can be made to the theory which holds that the various emotional disturbances are due to disturbances in the vascular innervation that accompanies the affections, and which, therefore, makes these vasomotor disturbances the only primary symptoms; (20) nevertheless, there still remains for us to investigate the problem whether those disturbances which are so obvious if they involve the blood vessels in the skin, by blushing or paling, by swelling or contracting, by heat or cold, are as obvious if they involve the inner organs, especially the central nervous system from which most of the other emotional phenomena spring (21). That this affection of the blood vessels occurs also in the nervous system is a necessary assumption for the theory that they are fundamental to the other disturbances of innervation. A priori, the assumption that the change in degree of contraction of the blood vessels during affection is not limited to the skin, but is spread all over the entire organism, is undoubtedly the most probable. There are, as we have already mentioned above, plenty of data, and I have proceeded from the assumption of some such general distribution of hyperaemia or anaemia in my explanation of the different phenomena of the affections. Nevertheless, it would be valuable if we could perform immediate observations and experiments by which the truth or fallacy of my point of view might be shown. But the number and value of such experiences leave much to be desired for our physiological insight. It is not easy to get rid of this inadequacy of empirical data, since experiments performed on animals are of little or no use in this field;[18] and in regard to human beings, we have so far been limited to drawing our conclusions from very rare cases, which require direct observation of the brain and its blood vessels, which, under normal conditions, possessed at least enough life to permit of changing dispositions.

Attempts have been made to measure the changes in the blood supply of the brain by temperature measurements outside of the head. This method can easily be applied to all individuals, in order to produce a wide range for the experiments. It has then been attempted to prove that an increase in temperature occurs following every mental effort, due to an increased blood flow to the brain. But, even if this method is indisputable, as it seems in fact to be, it can hardly have any application to the study of the affections, because the relations here change so rapidly that the sudden changes in circulation hardly endure long enough to vary the temperature outside of the head, and especially not in the case of individuals who know that they are under observation. And so our present immediate experiences of the blood-content of the brain during dispositional changes depend upon such cases, where rather large parts of the skull have been removed so that the brain, or its skins, are laid bare, but where the patient is nevertheless in a pretty normal mental condition. But the possibility of observing such a case is, however, not sufficient; in order to obtain results, one must have the good fortune to be present as observer at just that moment when the patient is disturbed naturally by a rather strong emotion, for of course it cannot be controlled artificially; and not every one knows how to appreciate the relations in question, especially the changes in pulsatory brain-movements.

Obviously, our present data are insignificant, and sufficient only

[18] There are a few series of experiments (v. Bezold, Danilevsky, Conty and Charpentier) which illustrate the change in blood pressure under the influence of the emotions, especially of fright, the only emotion which can be aroused experimentally, if need be. This influence is very obvious; a sudden fright results—even after severing the N. vagus—in increased blood-pressure in the large arteries, and that means a contraction of the fine blood-vessels, as we have assumed to be the case in the effect of fear on man.

to prove rather tentatively that emotions are in fact accompanied by disturbances in the brain circulation. Earlier observations of this fact have been made. The renowned English surgeon, Astley Cooper, who lived at the beginning of this century, had opportunity to observe a man, who suffered from a significant defect of the base of the skull, and declared that the pulsations of the brain were increased every time anything was said that displeased the patient. Several years ago, the Italian physiologist, Mosso,[19] made more accurate observations under similar conditions. A man, whose brain was laid open over a rather large area, showed that any insult or sensation of anger increased the pulsation of the brain, and also the pulse of the arteries in the arm, even though the activity of the heart did not seem to be affected in any way. One striking change in brain pulsation was evidenced at noon, when the chimes began to ring: this Mosso declared to be due to the fact that the patient was disturbed because he could not cross himself as usual to say his Ave Maria. On the whole, Mosso found that emotional disturbances affected the brain-circulation much more than thought-activity, no matter how great the effort.

According to all physiological experiences, nothing opposes the assumption that the immediate bodily expression of the affections is a change in the function of the vasomotor apparatus, different for each affection, and that the other bodily appearances, which accompany the affections, are due to these vaso-motor disturbances, these changes in the blood-content of the various organs, and members of the body. Thus the changes in appearance (skin) and in the functions (22) (nervous-system, secretory glands) of the organs are explained. The assumption of such a relation greatly simplifies the condition as a whole, and facilitates, as we shall soon see, the physiological comprehension, which would be difficult if we had to assume a direct primary origin for all these various phenomena. Besides, we must mention particularly that my fundamental conception of the psychology of the affections is in no way disturbed, if we should in future be forced to the last mentioned conception. So far, there is on hand so great a probability for a vasomotor theory, that we may proceed from its assumption.

[19] A. Mosso, *The Blood Circulation in the Human Brain.* 1881. p. 13.

We now face a problem of essential interest from a psycho-physiological point of view, and which therefore constitutes the main point of this investigation, namely: the question concerning the nature of the relation of the emotions to the concomitant body-phenomena.

So far, I have always, even if under protest, employed such phrases as "the physiological phenomena produced by emotions" or "the physiological phenomena which accompany the affections," in order, by using the popular expressions for the relation in question, to facilitate temporarily their comprehension. Strange to say this relation has never been defined even broadly; I know of no attempt made to establish its real nature. For the popular conception, the matter is very simple. The emotions are entities, substances, forces, demons, which attack human beings and cause physical as well as mental disturbances: "I was seized with sorrow," "I met with a great pleasure," "I was controlled by anger," "fear overwhelmed me," etc. (23); or one may substitute the more English expressions: "seized with anger," "in the clutches of fear." This naïve conception, which, like many other things in popular psychology and some in scientific psychology, owes its force only to a certain demonstrativeness, would hardly be recognized in modern psychology, if we could substitute a more comprehensible and exact explanation. Most modern authors of scientific psychology do not recognize this question at all;[20] in fact, they seem purposely to pass over it in silence, perhaps in order not to be forced—for lack of a physiological explanation—to have recourse to the code-language of speculative psychology. In fact, it may be said that even scientific psychology shares in the belief that the affections call forth, cause, the physical phenomena. But as to the real nature of the affections, that they can have such great influence upon the body, no word of explanation is to be found in all modern psychology—even in Wundt (*Physiological-psychology*, 2 ed., Vol. II, Ch. 33).

If a clear understanding of relations which I have discussed above is to be made possible, we must I think, put the facts in the

[20] The external motions are always due to internal emotions (Wundt, Concerning the Expression of Emotions, *Deutsche Rundschau*, April, 1877).

following form: We have in every emotion as sure and tangible factors: (1) a cause—a sensory impression which usually is modified by memory or a previous associated image; and (2) an effect— namely, the above mentioned vaso-motor changes and consequent changes in bodily and mental functions. And now we have the question: What lies between these two factors; or does anything lie between them? If I start to tremble when I am threatened with a loaded pistol, does a purely mental process arise, fear, which is what causes my trembling, palpitation of the heart, and confusion; or are these bodily phenomena aroused immediately by the frightening cause, so that the emotion consists exclusively of these functional disturbances of the body?

The answer to this question is obviously not only of far-reaching significance in the psychology of the affections, but also of the greatest practical importance for every physician who has anything to do with the pathological results of violent emotions.

The popular opinion seems to be that, as has been mentioned, the immediate outcome of a situation which arouses an emotion is a purely psychic one, that is, either a new power is generated in the mind, or a modification of the mental condition takes place; and furthermore, that this mental activity is the actual affection, the real pleasure, pain, etc., whereas the physical phenomena are merely secondary, always present, to be sure, but in themselves quite unessential.

The purely mental affection is a hypothesis and, like every hypothesis, is justified only if (1) it explains the phenomena it is assumed to explain, and (2) it is necessary for the explanation of these phenomena.

In regard to the first of the above requirements, the questionable hypothesis has as good chances as any hypothesis of speculative science. Without objections being offered by experience, hypotheses can be broadened at will and they can be endowed with any attribute or power, and consequently they serve any purpose which may be required of them. Can mental fear explain why we turn pale and tremble? Even though we do not understand that, we are free to assume it to be true, and as a rule that is sufficient for us.

If the hypothesis of the psychical nature of the affections, there-fore, is indisputable in this point, especially because it lies outside of the realm of proof, the question arises whether it fulfills the second requirement; to be necessary for the explanation of that group of phenomena which we call affections, so that they cannot be understood without its help.

If anyone were to dispute it, if, for example, some one attempted to prove to a man who has grown up with the popular conception of this problem that when he is frightened, his fear is only a percep-tion of the changes in his body, he would very probably meet with the following objection first:—"The assumption of this relation is disproved by personal experience, for fear, like every emotion, has a distinct sensation of a peculiar change, a specific condition of the mind, quite independent of the body." I can well under-stand how this objection may appear very significant to most people, and be difficult to refute, and yet it has obviously no value whatever, in and for itself, since we have absolutely no immediate means of differentiating between a sensation of mental and one of physical nature. No man, in fact, is capable of differentiating between a sensation of mental and one of physical nature. No man, in fact, is capable of differentiating between psychical and somatic feelings. Whoever attributes a sensation to the mind, does so only on basis of theory, not on basis of immediate percep-tion. I have no doubt that a mother who mourns the death of her child would resent, yes, be indignant, if any one were to tell her that what she feels: the weariness and laxity of her muscles, the coldness of her bloodless skin, the impossibility of her brain to concentrate in clear, quick thought;[21] may be attributed to an image of the cause of these phenomena. But this is no ground for indignation, for her feeling is just as strong, just as deep and pure, if attributed to one as to the other cause. It cannot exist, how-ever, without its physical attributes.

[21] I will not delay to consider the objection which might be offered, namely, that a purely mental sorrow, joy, etc., can be experienced when-ever the affection is not strong enough to cause bodily symptoms. Such an assumption obviously rests upon very incomplete observation, or upon this, that purely subjective sensations—of lightness or of pressure, of strength or weakness—are considered psychical.

Take away the bodily symptoms from a frightened individual; let his pulse beat calmly, his look be firm, his color normal, his movements quick and sure, his speech strong, his thoughts clear; and what remains of his fear?

If, therefore, we cannot rely upon the testimony of personal, subjective experiences in this question because they are incompetent here, nevertheless the question is by no means cleared up. Even if this hypothesis of psychical affections is not made necessary by subjective experiences, it may still be indispensable, since perhaps we cannot understand how the bodily phenomena of the affections arise[22] without it.

And so, next we have to examine whether the physical expressions of affections may arise in a purely physical way; if this be the case, then the necessity of the hypothesis is obviated.

As a matter of fact, it is not difficult to prove now, and by means of the most ordinary and well known experiences, that emotions may be induced by a variety of causes which are utterly independent of disturbances of the mind, and that, on the other hand, they may be suppressed and modified by pure physical means. The fact that our whole manner of living, our daily diet, has developed in the course of generations with this aim in view, to favor the pleasant affections and to modify or entirely remove the unpleasant ones, is very well accepted, even if without clear consciousness of the actual connection of things. I will offer only one example: it will suffice to recall many. It is one of the oldest experiences of mankind that "wine gladdens the heart" and the power of alcoholic liquors to reduce sorrow and fear and to substitute joy and courage has found application, which is in and for itself natural enough, and would be most wholesome, if the substance did not produce other effects in addition.

We all understand "why Jeppe drinks."[23] He seeks to free himself from his marital troubles and his fear of Master Erich, and

[22] It is hardly necessary to point out that the assumption of processes in the mind for the explanation of the physical symptoms for a scientific conception is in reality only another expression for the fact that the origin of these symptoms is still a mystery to us.

[23] Jeppe am Berge. Character in a classic comedy by Holberg (note added by Kurella).

he wishes once again to sing and recall the happy past when he was still "with Maliz." Brandy makes him gay and brave, without requiring even a single brightening or enlivening impression, which might act directly upon his mind, and without causing him to forget his cares or his enemies in the least. He wants only to look at them from another point of view, under the influence of brandy; he wants to impress the sexton and to beat his wife again; for alcohol has excited his vasomotor apparatus, has increased the speed and strength of his heart-beats, has dilated his capillaries, thereby increasing his innervation enough to make him chatter loudly, sing and row, instead of dragging himself over the road, moaning and whining. He receives a sensation of warmth, levity and power, instead of his customary laxity and incompetence. His dull brain wakes up under the influence of heightened circulation, thoughts begin to come to him, old memories appear and drive away the habitual feeling of misery, and all for one peg of brandy, whose effect on the circulation we can understand and which requires no intervention of the mind to affect the vasomotor centers.

All those who drink brandy bear a similar relation to it, and we possess this relation to our daily luxuries and comforts, and to our various arrangements which we make to ensure our comfort and convenience. So long as we find ourselves in the easy, accustomed path of our daily life, the relation of our emotions to material influences (for example, to nourishment) is, of course, not so obvious. A different relation obtains when certain substances are partaken of, substances which have such a strong effect on the system that they are used either as medicines or belong to the category of poisons. This is well known in the case of certain mushrooms, especially of the toad-stool, which call forth violent outbreaks of rage and brutality in whoever partakes of them. Our belligerent ancestors are supposed to have used them to get into the proper spirit for the "Berserk rage," just as we today "take a drink" to "get up" our courage. Attacks of rage may also occur after using Hashish (Indian hemp), which as a rule, only stimulates the system to unrestrained joyfulness in much the same way that alcohol does.

Certain sickening drugs, such as tartar emetic, ipecacuanha, etc., have a depressing effect, which is in some respects comparable to fear and sorrow, and, like these, is accompanied by phenomena of collapse.

If emotional states can be induced by taking certain substances, or in any other purely physical way, it follows that troublesome affections can be counteracted and modified in a similar way. If brandy or opium induces joy, then they will oppose sorrow, etc.

The power of a "cold shower" to dampen violence and wrath sometimes finds practical application, and yet this method can hardly have any direct effect upon the mind, if applied *in natura;* so much the stronger is the effect upon the vasomotor functions. By means of one drug—the well-known potassium bromide— which has a paralyzing effect on the vasomotor apparatus, we have it in our power not only to allay fear and sorrow and other similar unpleasant affections, but also to induce a condition of apathy, which makes it impossible for the subject to be either lively or depressed, fearful or angry, simply because the vasomotor functions have been suspended.

If the conception of the nature of the affections as here represented is established, then we may expect that every influence involving general changes in the vascular nervous system must have an emotional expression. Of course, we cannot expect that these emotions will coincide exactly with the phenomena for which we usually reserve this denotation; the differences in cause will naturally result in various effects. The various psychical causes also have effects which are not at all congruent. Fear of a ghost, for example, does not manifest itself in the same way as the fear of the guns of the enemy. Nevertheless, the similarity between physically and mentally induced affections has, in many cases, deen so conspicuous as to force the immediate conception, as many verbal expressions prove. We have the same expression for mental and physical pain in many languages: their great physiological similarity has been recognized, although the eminent characteristic of physical pain, the subjective sensation resulting from the transference of the peripheral stimulation to the sensory center, is entirely absent in mental pain. The cause of the similarity to emotional pain is the reflexive innervation of the vascular nerves, a regular effect of every strong stimulation of the sensory nerves.

In the same way "shudder" is used in speech for both the effect of sudden cold upon the skin, and for phenomena due to impressions from fright. That this naïve conception knows no difference between emotional and purely physical "shudders" is evident from the story of the boy who set out to "get a thrill," and after he had tried in vain to "thrill" in the presence of dead and of ghosts, finally obtained his wish when he was thrown out of his bed into a tub of cold water. This produced a far stronger effect upon his vasomotor appartus than did the sight of death-beds or ghosts. To call a man "feverish" who suffers great suspense is another example of how striking is the similarity between the slight symptoms of fever which are induced chiefly by vasomotor disturbances, and those physical conditions which are caused by anxious expectation, etc. (24).

As has been mentioned, I do not wish to enter upon the great problem of the relation of the affections to actual pathological conditions, and to psychical and physical diseases.

But one relation does obtain here, which I cannot quite pass over, because it will throw great light upon the question, so vital to us, of the necessity of the hypothesis of purely mental affections. If anything can prove absolutely the dispensibility of this hypothesis, it certainly must be the fact that affections which influence our psychical life are induced without any external influence or circumstance, and aside from memory or association of ideas; and that they occur *in optima forma* on the mere basis of conditions of disease which develop in the body or are inherited.

If we proceed from the conception represented here, this cannot appear strange to us; for, of course, the vasomotor apparatus may also be affected by disease at times, just like any other part of the nervous system, and be caused to function abnormally, or to be put out of commission entirely. We may consider it especially exposed to the danger of abnormal functioning, because it is a part of the nervous system, which enjoys less rest and is more frequently attacked by functional disturbances than any other organ. Wherever this occurs, the patient becomes either depressed, or raging, terrified, or excessively lively, or embarrassed, etc., all without motive, even though he is conscious of not having any reason for his anger, his fear or joy. What support can we find here for an assumption of "mental affections?"

Such cases are extraordinarily common. Every psychiatrist knows the sharply defined characteristics which occur in melancholia or mania. Every physician, who is interested in nervous diseases, has plenty of opportunity to observe the still more instructive cases which lie on the border between real insanity and mere "indispositions," which come under the head of "irritability," "eccentricity," "dejection," etc. Most frequently we find "dejection" (the image of sorrow or even of despair), which often leads to suicide in spite of the full, clear consciousness that there is absolutely no mental motive for sorrow. Less frequent is the diseased condition of fear, which is often combined with related affection, with sorrow, but also occurs alone. Sometimes we also find that joy occurs in disease; the mere fact that joy appears unmotivated and without cause is not sufficient proof for the layman to consider it diseased, and still less to suggest medical treatment.

It is usually necessary for the joy to express itself most unrestrainedly as a more or less decided mania, or that it alternate in a striking manner with periods of depression: circumstances which cause it to appear abnormal. The same holds true of anger. As regards this affection, we are wont to accept much that presupposes no corresponding pathological condition, and we are not as particular regarding the motivation. However, everything has its limits and frequently there are outbreaks of anger which have so little motive, and are so unbridled, that all will agree in considering them expressions of a pathological condition.

There is perhaps nothing that can be more enlightening to a non-medical man than the observation of such a pathological attack of rage, especially if it appears unmodified by any other psychic disturbances, as happens rarely, by the way, in the so-called "transitory mania" form of disease. Often the attack comes without the slightest provocation to predisposed patients, who are otherwise quite rational, and puts them (to speak with the latest writer[24] on the subject) in condition of "wild paroxysms

[24] O. Schwartzer, *Die transitorische Tobsucht*. Wien, 1880.

of rage, with a terrible, blind raving impulse to destruction and violence." The patient suddenly attacks his surroundings, strikes, stamps his feet, kicks, crushes everything he can lay hands on, throws down everything he can get hold of, smashes and tears to pieces whatever is near him, tears his clothes, screams, yells, howls and rolls his gleaming eyes and shows all symptoms of vasomotor congestion that we have become acquainted with before in rage. The face is reddened, swollen, the cheeks are hot, the eyes protrude and their choroids become bloodshot, the beat of the heart increases, and the pulse beats 100 to 120 times a minute. The arteries of the neck swell and pulsate, the veins swell, salivation is increased. The attack lasts only a few hours and comes to a sudden end in an 8 to 12 hour sleep, and the patient on awakening has forgotten all that happened.

The pathological affections discussed above are due to physical abnormalities and may appear either as symptoms of other diseases, or because of some disturbance in metabolism or digestion, etc. Hence, they are influenced by purely material therapy and may be improved and cured thereby. The above quoted case of transitory mania, which obviously is due to a sudden congestion in the brain can sometimes, according to the above quoted author, be cured by ice compresses around the head (25).

Here I foresee one objection, which I do not wish to pass over unnoticed, in spite of its weakness logically. Undoubtedly many, in agreement with daily usage of speech, will say: "The conditions which are brought about by purely physical influences, or by diseased conditions of the body, may look like affections, but are not."

The raving caused by a toadstool, for example, or by mania, may have the same appearance as rage, but is not the real rage, just as little as the joy which comes of drinking wine is not real joy; therefore, in absence of a mental joy, in cases of toadstool poisoning, or mania, we cannot conclude that no such purely mental state exists, if rage is as a rule caused by a mental impression.

Now, it is easy to comprehend that such a division of affections into real and apparent, such a limiting of the range of "real affections," is quite consciously based upon a *petitio principii*. The reason for suggesting that such a group of the "real affections" is due to purely mental influences, is the only possible assumption that can be made, in which the disposition (*Gemüth*) is involved. But that is precisely the point of this investigation.

In reality, the difference between the Berserk-madness of a man poisoned by a toad-stool, the maniacal-madness and the rage of one who has suffered a bloody insult, lies only in the difference of cause and in the consciousness of the respective causes, or in the lack of consciousness of a cause. If we want to differentiate between these differences, there is, of course, no objection to offer; only it must be clearly understood wherein the difference lies.

Indeed, it is not so easy to draw a line between material and mental causes for affections; and if we try to sound the physiological differences, they vanish into something quite insignificant physiologically, and slip through our fingers. It has never occurred to anyone to separate the emotion due to a suddenly discharged shot, from the true affections. No one hesitates to call it fright, and it presents all the ordinary characteristics of fright. Nevertheless, it has no connection with any image of danger, and is not caused by any association of ideas, memory, or any other mental process. The phenomena of fright follow the shot immediately, without any trace of "mental" fright. Many will never grow accustomed to standing beside a gun when it is fired, merely on account of the noise, although they know perfectly well that there is no danger present, either to them or to any one else. We can also consider the case of the infant, which presents all the phenomena of fright at every strong impression of sound; we cannot assume that the sound arouses an image of danger in this case.

Here, where we must assume that the pure vasomotor reflex is released by a direct circuit from the center of hearing, if not indirectly by the auditory nerves, we have an emotion of purely material origin.[25] And so, we must either exclude this fright from

---

[25] It is not probable that this is a case of a pure, simple reflex of the motor nerves, as Preyer, for example, seems to assume (*Die Seele des Kindes*, 2d ed., p. 51), partly because the apparent movements do not look as if they were caused by a sudden impression that releases a reflex, partly, also, because the effects are not limited to the motor phenomena.

the real affections, or we cannot support the differentiation between mentally and physically induced affections. We meet with the same difficulty in the case of the usually less intense, but nevertheless sufficiently decided, emotions that are aroused by simple impressions made upon other sense organs, which have no connection with any association of ideas; the pleasure we take in a pretty color, or color combination, our repulsion towards a bad taste or odor, discomfort in pain.

If we have begun to feel uncertain about the establishment of a border line between the mental and physical causes of affections, we will discover a strong impulse to examine what physiological significance this difference possesses, *i.e.*, what difference exists in the cerebral mechanism of emotions, in the brain activity when the cause is mental and when it is purely material.

In the face of our present still incomplete knowledge of the physiology of the brain, it is of course not very tempting to attempt an explanation of what happens in the brain in mental activity. It of course can be only a question of the crudest fundamental outlines, and with every qualification regarding the accuracy of the results. Nevertheless, in physiological investigations, it is not only justified, but even correct and desirable to determine definitely just what can be done in the light of our present physiological knowledge. At least, we may derive encouragement from the fact that these relations as described here are very easy to grasp, in their fundamental outlines.

Whatever the causes may be that arouse affections, the effects on the nervous system are identical in one point; in the effect upon the vasomotor center, that group of nerve cells which regulates the innervation of the bloodvessels. The stimulation of these cells, which lie chiefly in the part of the cord between the brain and the spinal cord, is the root of the causes of the affections, however else they may be constituted; and is fundamental to the physiological phenomena which are the essential components of the affections. But the paths which lead thither are various, according to the nature of the causes, not only according to whether they enter by one or another sense-organ, but also according to whether they are simple sense impressions, or complicated, so-called psychic processes. It seems that for the formation of those emotions which are due to a simple sense impression, a loud noise, a beautiful color combination, etc., the path to the vaso-motor center must be quite direct, and the cerebral mechanism but slightly complicated. Consider $\emptyset$ to be the sense organ in the following figure, the eye for example, which received the impression in question and which subsequently passes along the optic nerve ($N.O.$) to the central optic organ ($C.O.'$), is diverted by a simple nerve connection to the vasomotor center ($C.V.$) to lead off the impulse first aroused in the eye and in this way to effect the emotional changes in the vascular innervation (26).

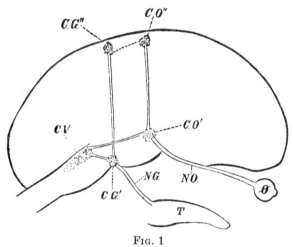

FIG. 1

The matter becomes somewhat more complicated when those affections are involved which are produced not by a simple impression upon some sense-organ, but by some "mental process," some memory or association of ideas, even if the latter be due to sense-impression. Such causes usually produce a much stronger emotional effect than do the simple sense-impressions. The latter usually only arouse affections when they are very powerful, and their effects are usually not so deep nor so lasting, especially when compared with those aroused psychically.

Fortunately, things are arranged so that most sense-impressions are entirely without emotional effects, and that they obtain such effects only by stimulation through mental activity. When

I begin to tremble, if threatened by a loaded gun, it is evidently not the sense-impression which causes the fear, for a loaded gun looks just like an empty one, which I would not have noticed at all. What, then, happens in the brain, when an affection is induced by a sense impression that can have no direct effect upon the vascular nerve center as can a loud report, etc.? In order possibly to give a somewhat adequate answer to this question, we must proceed from the consideration of the simplest imaginable case. There are undoubtedly an infinite number of possibilities which are for the most part very complicated and impossible of analysis. But, on the other hand, a very simple case contributes by its suggestion of the relation, to the solution of this complicated problem for future physiological research.

As an example of the simplest type, I shall offer the following case, for the correctness of which every mother would testify. A young child will cry at the sight of the spoon which has previously been used several times to give him nasty medicine; how does that happen? Such a case, or analogous ones, are frequently cited from the psychological point of view, and very diverse answers will be found for our question. "He cries, because he considers the spoon to be the cause of his former distress," we say. But this does not help to explain the fact. Or he cries "because the spoon reawakens memories of former sufferings," which may be quite true, but does not transfer the case to the field of physiology; or "because the spoon arouses fear of future discomforts;" but the question is, just how does the sight of the spoon arouse fear because of its previous use, *i.e.*, how is it capable of setting the vaso-motor center in action in a certain way?

Whenever the child received medicine from that spoon, his visual sense was stimulated as well as his gustatory sense, by the sight of the spoon as well as by the taste of the medicine. Both impressions are conveyed to the brain from the peripheral sense organs, and there, after they have become sensations in the central sense organ (in $C.G.'$ and $C.O.'$ in the above figure), they are brought to consciousness in that they are brought to the centers of taste and vision in the cortex (in $C.G.''$ and $C.O.''$). But the dispositional outbreaks of the child show conclusively that each impression of taste is always conveyed to the vaso-motor center

($C.V.$ from $C.G.'$) and hereby arouses the phenomena which express fright, disgust, et al. The sight of the spoon alone therefore can not set the vascular nerves in action; if we show the spoon to a child in a condition of ignorance, before he has tasted the bitters that he may receive from it, he will reach for it instead of beginning to cry.

But if he has seen the spoon in action a few times, and has noticed that this sight is always followed by a disgusting taste, it becomes evident that the sight of the spoon alone has the power to make the child cry, $i.e.$, to stimulate his vasomotor center to activity. This must now be capable of being aroused either from the point $C.O.'$ or from the point $C.O.''$, which before had no influence whatever.

From which of these points now does the impulse to $C.V.$ start, when the child sees the hated spoon? Surely from $C.O.''$, the cortical center, since this is the first organ where an image of the spoon becomes conscious. Now it is a question why the group of cells $C.O.''$, which formerly had no influence upon the vasomotor center, is now capable of stimulating it to emotional activity. When we recall that the fact that visual and gustatory impressions have been received simultaneously numerous times is the cause, we begin to think immediately that a functional connection must have been established by these simultaneous stimulations between the two cell groups $C.O.''$ and $C.G.''$, the conscious centers for the appearance of the spoon and the taste of the medicine; so we must add that whenever $C.O.''$ are activated by the sight of the spoon, the impulse is conducted to $C.G.''$, from whence again, as is evident in view of the well known power of memory to arouse emotions, it is easily conducted to $C.V.$[26] I fear that the assumption of a new, so far untried, functional relation between $C.G.''$ and $C.O.''$ must, at first sight, look like one of the many subterfuges which physiological psychology does not always scorn

[26] Whether this takes place over the paths $C.G.''$–$C.G.'$ and $C.G.'$–$C.V.$, or over other unknown ones, cannot be determined. But there is no reason to object to the above mentioned courses, for they also take care of a reversed direction, since the reversible conduction of the nerve fibers, which obviously cannot be observed in the peripheral nerves, certainly must play an important part in the central organs, when their amphicellular arrangement favors and necessitates it.

to make use of in its theories. It is temptingly easy to "open new roads" by a pen-stroke, when we wish to have something done between two points in the brain, which before have possessed no relation. If then we consider such "roads" to be represented by nerve-fibers, we certainly build on a very shaky hypothesis; for, outside of early evolutionary periods, we have no proof of the condition that nerve fibers which formerly have been inert will begin activity. But the matter is different, if we consider the conduction of an impulse from one place to another by means of connected nerve-cells, as we would have to assume the path of conduction between $C.O.''$ and $C.G.''$ to be. The numerous phenomena of irradiation, ordinary and pathological, demonstrate adequately that the "blazing of the trail" easily takes place under these conditions as a result of repeated stimulation of one or the other cell group.

But we must not be satisfied with such an indeterminate representation like the one contained in the expression "to blaze a new trail." We must make it clear to ourselves, how this relation is to be understood in each individual case; the new connection between the two points may be established in a number of different ways.

In the above case, we see that the point $C.G.''$ which originally was not stimulated when an impulse reached $C.O.''$, now is activated by an impression received at $C.O.''$, after both points have been simultaneously stimulated a few times. If we were to say now, that this is a simple phenomenon of irradiation; the stimulation at $C.O.''$ spreads, irradiates by means of cell connections to $C.G.''$; nothing would, in fact, be explained, for it would still remain a mystery just what leads the irradiation to $C.G.''$, as we can assume beforehand that the phenomenon can take place in any direction from $C.O.''$, with equal ease. Our supposition does not justify our assuming that the process of irradiation takes place in one direction only, although this is very possible. We must proceed from the theory that it radiates from $C.O.''$ in all directions, and decreases in intensity with the distance from this point.

What has occurred in the above case is not a "blazing of a new trail" in the sense of opening paths which have not been traversed before. The new effect of this sense-impression upon the child does not depend upon his being led along new paths, which formerly were closed, but upon the fact that the point $C.G.''$ is in a condition to be influenced by the irradiation from the point $C.O.''$, more strongly than any other group of cells which may be affected; or rather, $C.G.''$ is the only group which responds recognizably to the impulse propagated by irradiation.

We can only consider the fact that this group has previously been stimulated simultaneously with $C.O.''$ as a reason for this greater sensitivity. A change has hereby been produced in its cells, a condition of excitability, which is not to be found in the other brain cells, which may be reached by irradiation. A summation of functional activity occurs in $C.G.''$ due to the existing activity and the additional activity conducted to it from $C.O.''$[27] The reason for the fact that $C.G.''$ is only stimulated by irradiation coming from $C.O.''$, and not by that coming from any other point in the cortex, is quite easily explained. But an investigation of this point would require trespassing in other fields of psychophysiology. Therefore, I pass over the question, and that the more willingly, since it is here only a question of sketching the main direction of the path over which we can conceive the process of stimulation of the vasomotor centers to pass, wherever it is a question of an indirect "mental" affection.

The exemplary case quoted above, as has been mentioned, has been taken as simple and as uncomplicated as possible. Of course, the process is much more complicated in most indirect affections; in other words, the impulse coming from outside must traverse a much more round-about path in the brain, must pass more stations, before it reaches the vasomotor center (27); but the outlines of the physiological procedure will essentially remain

[27] This relation will perhaps become clearer when we recall the phenomena of interference, which shows that one wave motion may be reinforced by another wave of the same nature. The irradiation which proceeds from the point $C.O.''$ and which spreads with decreasing intensity in all directions may be compared to the circular wave motion set up when a stone is thrown into a pool of still water. If, now, one of the disturbances coming from $C.O.''$ meets a similar one that has started earlier, but which is still active and coming from $C.G.''$, then the tract between may be set into stronger motion by interference than any other ray from $C.O.''$

constant: a conduction of the stimulation from the cells of the central sense organs to the cortical cells, and from these finally to the vasomotor cells in the mid-brain.

And, so, I probably was justified in my statement (on page 72) that the difference between emotions induced by material and mental methods was not absolute, not even essential, from a physiological point of view. The chief requisites for formation remains the same for both, the stimulation of the vasomotor centers; the difference lies in the path which the impulse pursues to reach this center. To this we must still add the fact that an increase of impulse occurs in the case of indirect, "mental" affections, due to a previous brain stimulation which has not yet quite died away, and the effect of which is added to the impulse coming from the external impression.

I hope that it will now be obvious that, as I have already remarked in the introduction, the problem is reversed, if we, as often has been done in the past, and as still happens, set out to determine the physiological and pathological effects of affections upon the body.

The statement of the problem is wrong in principle, for the emotions are not forces which stand outside of the body and control it, and whoever proceeds conscientiously in his investigation will soon come to the conclusion that this problem is practically insolvable. If, nevertheless, it has been believed that it is possible to offer a thousand answers to the question of the influence of joy and sorrow, of fright and anger, etc., upon the pshsiological expressions of life, only a quite aιbitrary and impossible schematization has been obtained, by which every phenomenon which did not fit into the scheme was excluded. And so I too have proceeded in the above sketch of the bodily expressions of the affections. Anyone who has followed this sketch will easily see that it holds good only for certain cases which we will call the typical, or better still, the conventional ones, because it is they that have gradually assumed in the course of time a kind of symbolic significance in art and literature, representing groups of related phenomena. But we have all seen people struck dumb with joy, rather than made loquacious, we have seen fright rush the blood to the head of its victim, instead of making him turn pale, and have seen the mourner rush about restless and moaning, rather than silent and dejected, etc. This is natural, for the same cause may have a different effect upon the vascular nerves of different people, since these do not always give the same reaction in different individuals, and besides, the impulse has been influenced by various factors previous to its path through the brain, under the psychological form of memories and associated ideas. But he who states the problem in the traditional form must do violence to the facts in another respect, namely, in a conscious schematization of the affections, an establishment of definite forms; whereas in reality a multitude of unnoticeable transitions occur. That is a deliberate act, which is perhaps more flagrant than would be the establishing of seven definite colors to represent the entire range of colors. Such an act might be permissible in daily speech, but is quite out of the question in a scientific investigation, where it can only happen by trespassing and neglecting all the innumerable shades of transition, which so far have no name in speech.

How often are we not embarrassed when called upon to decide how to classify our momentary disposition under the conventional headings? How often must we not be satisfied with vague expressions for some emotional process ("I became excited," "I was irritated," "my disposition was upset," etc.), and be unable to bring it under any one affection that has a name in the language?

The truly scientific problem in this field is the determination of the emotional reaction of the vasomotor system to various influences. The solution of this problem is still a long ways off. The present investigation goes no further than to point out the problem.

We owe all the emotional side of our mental life, our joys and sorrows, our happy and unhappy hours, to our vasomotor system. If the impressions which fall upon our senses did not possess the power of stimulating it, we would wander through life unsympathetic and passionless, all impressions of the outer world would only enrich our experience, increase our knowledge, but would arouse neither joy nor anger, would give us neither care nor fear (28).

It is true of the vasomotor apparatus as well as of all parts of the nervous system, that its irritability is very different for different people. In some, it is easily stimulated and reacts to comparatively slight impulses.

Everyday experience teaches how much more easily some individuals' hearts palpitate than others; how much more easily some blush or pale; how some are more sensitive to heat and cold; and we all know that those individuals whose vasomotor systems are so easily stimulated are the ones who easily become violent and angry, or excessively joyful, etc. Not only individual, but also inherited differences frequently occur here; more general and frequently highly significant relations play a part. Women, whose nervous system and especially the vasomotor division, proves to be much more sensitive than that of men, are much oftener the prey of affections than is the other sex. The same analogy holds true for children in comparison with adults. As is well known, racial peculiarities may cause differences, and since we cannot learn very much about the difference in sensitivity of the vasomotor systems of the various races, we may be allowed to reverse the conclusion and consider the greater or lesser mobility of the vascular nerves in response to a given stimulus. On account of the perspective into the future which it gives, one circumstance deserves particular notice, namely that individuals as well as races are subject to a greater degree of emotion the lower their position in society.

The so-called savage races, when racial peculiarities do not act in the opposite direction, are more violent and unrestrained, more excessive in their joy, more subjugated by sorrow, than civilized nations. The same difference occurs between the various generations of one and the same race; we are calm and tame compared to our barbarian ancestors, whose greatest delight lay in working themselves up to an insane rage for battle, but who, on the other hand, were so depressed by misfortune as to end their lives for a mere bagatelle. And, finally, we see a similar difference existing between the various classes of society in the same generation. The surest sign of "refinement" is the self-control with which educated persons bear misfortunes that would call forth outbreaks of passion in the uneducated.

This repression of emotion during the progressive education of individuals and of generations proceeds hand in hand, not only with advancing development of mental life, but is also a result of this development.

Mental life, too, is dependant upon vasomotor function, though in a somewhat different manner from emotional life. Intellectual operations cause, and are due to, an increase of blood supply to the brain, naturally, to parts of the brain other than those which are especially involved in emotions.

To a certain degree a contradiction exists between the mental life and the emotional. The former acts "derivatively" (in the original sense of the word), conducting the blood away from the latter; and when Hermann von Bremen counts twenty, he relieves the motor part of his brain of such an amount of blood by this bit of intellectual activity that he no longer feels the impulse to strike.[28]

Education acts along the same lines. The aim of all education, (which must not be confused with instruction) is to increase self-control and the opposition or suppression of impulses, which are the immediate effects of our bodily organization, but which do not fit into established social conditions. Physiologically, we consider education to consist in practice in the ability to control simple elementary reflexes by higher ones. We are taught from earliest childhood to control the vasomotor reflexes of emotions and other reflexes not fitting for decent society. A child is punished when he starts to cry as a result of emotional vascular convulsions, just as much as when he does not keep himself clean, because of the uncontrolled reflexes of his bladder.

In the course of years, the center of the vascular nerves loses more and more of its emotional activity by reason of the influence of control and lack of practice, and, as we have discovered so often in acquired characters, this result of development of the mental life and of education is transmitted to posterity by inheritance; generations arise which have less and less prompt emotional vascular innervation, and with always slighter innervation of the vascular nerves for the organs of intelligence. If our development continues to progress along these lines, we shall finally reach

[28] Hermann V. Br., a hero of the Holberg classical comedy, always counted twenty after his wife had struck him a blow, and he was then in a position to remain calm (note by Kurella).

Kant's ideal of the "man of pure reason," who will consider every affection, every joy and sadness, fear and fright, as a disease, a mental disturbance, which is not proper for him.

ADDENDA

(1) In the older philosophical terminology, the word *"passiones"* was used for both groups of phenomena. Thus, Descartes recognizes six *primitivae passiones"*: "astonishment, love, hate, desire, joy and sorrow (*De passionibus Art. 69*), and does not differentiate between the two kinds of psychical phenonena. Similarly, Spinoza uses the word *"affectus"* in a like manner. His five kinds are: desire, joy, sorrow, astonishment, scorn (*Ethics* ps. III, *De origine et natura affectum*). Later, however, attempts began to be made to establish a certain difference between *affectus* and *passiones*—passions—and to make affections correspond to our emotions and "passions" to our passions. Kant differentiates between affections and passions (*passiones animi*), but does not divide the phenomena under these heads. He considers love, hope, modesty, to be affections just like joy and sorrow. And although there is a tendency in later psychological usage to assign to *"passiones"* a definition which approximately corresponds to the German "Gemüthsbewegung," and the French and English *"emotions,"* which we are dealing with here, yet we find even in the most recent works of the most rigorous scientific character that *"Passion"* and *"Emotion"* *"Gemüthsbewegung,"* *"Affect"* and *"Leidenschaft"* are used rather interchangeably, with no attempt at differentiation of the individual psychical disturbances.

One author alone, the court-physician Lion, has made an attempt to differentiate between affections and passions (affections and passions from the point of view of modern science and of the legislature of 1866). After he justly bemoaned the fact of this general confusion, he established a series of diagnostic characteristics for both, but meeting, it seems to me, with no greater success than every other attempt at definition which proceeds from that unfortunate realistic conception to which our science is still wedded.

(2) A sharp, and therefore scientific, differentiation can, of course, only be reached as a conclusion to a scientific investigation of the emotional phenomena. For immediate application here, it is fortunately not of the least importance to have a detailed differentiation between the two groups of phenomena as a starting point. We are only interested in obtaining homogeneous material for our investigation, and that is not difficult since we can ourselves make the differentiation between the psychic phenomena that are involved in our investigation.

(3) Kant bases his definition of affections as sensations which (contrary to passions) permit of no consideration, whether we surrender ourselves to them, or whether we oppose them, on the part that reflection plays in passion. (*Anthropologie*, book 3, §70).

(4) In older psychological writers, we may still meet with attempts to define the individual emotions; but we find no explanation of the nature of the affections in these definitions. As a rule, they are purely causal, like those of Descartes, who defines joy as *"jucunda commotio animae in qua consistit possessio boni quod impressiones cerebri ei repraesentant ut suum (l. c.* Art. 91); and so he attributes joy to a consciousness of the possession of good; but about what joy itself really is, he says nothing. In the same way, Kant: when he defines modesty as fear due to anxious scorn of a person present (*Anthropologie*, book 3, §79). A definition like Spinoza's: *"Laetitia est hominis transitio a minore ad majorem perfectionem"* (*Ethics* ps. III), is purely nominal.

(5) In Denmark, we find the brief and superficial presentation of Professor Klingberg's in the *"Skandinavisk Literaturselskabs Skrifter,"* 9 *de Aargang*, 1813. More thorough and detailed is the work of Sibbern in his book, *"Om Forholdet mellem Sjäel og Legeme,"* 1849. Also, the work of A. Sell (*"Om Betydn. af. Sindsbevaegels. Som Sygdomsaarsager*, 1884). This deals chiefly with the pathological relations.

(6) I have (*cf.* Lecture on the pathology of the spinal cord, *Forlaesn over Rygmarvens Patol.*, p. 455 ff.) used the term "patent innervation" to describe a phenomenon which is very significant for the understanding of many pathological symptoms, but which so far has not been noticed by physiologists and pathologists. For, besides the obvious impulses from the brain, which control the so-called voluntary muscles, there are other continuous motor impulses which, as a rule, are not observed under normal conditions, because they are so slight that they do not effect an actual contraction of the muscles, but only cause a slight tension. Thus, our muscles suffer a slight contraction, even when at rest, as in sleep, so that our body usually assumes a position in sleep which it could not hold in death.

(7) A heightened activity of the constrictor apparatus of the blood-vessels (vascular spasm, vascular convulsion) may, as a rule, only cause a contraction of the smaller vessels, whose thin walls possess a relatively strong muscular coat. The consequence of a vascular convulsion is a change in the distribution of the blood in the vessels, so that the large vessels, which are not contracted, are over-filled with blood, whereas the smaller ones receive less blood than usual, or are even so completely contracted as to allow no blood to enter.

(8) I am myself not so sure of the truth of my above explanation of the apparent paradox that a sorrowful person weeps. We might also

assume that weeping is the effect of a spasmodic dilatation of the blood-vessels, and the profuse secretions which so frequently cause the swelling and reddening of the fleshy parts of the face are facts in favor of the assumption, this spasmodic dilation occurring frequently in sorrow, instead of the usual contraction. Physiological and pathological experiments prove adequately that one and the same vascular nerves may be caused to contract or dilate by the same stimulus, and we can discover no reason for the different effects.

(9) That an overwhelming sorrow can turn the hair gray very rapidly, over night, is an old experience, and we have reliable observations of the phenomenon of recent date. An experienced and keen observer, our well-known psychiatrist Selmer, with whom I was discussing the subject, was inclined to attribute the rapid turning gray of the hair, especially of women, after violent emotion, to the fact that they no longer took the trouble to conceal the gray hairs under the others so carefully, and he has often noticed that the original color returned as soon as the patients regained their normal self-control. It may be, of course, that this explanation is adequate for certain cases, especially in such cases where the hair literally turns gray "over night." Such a sudden change defies all explanation, even if we consider the only existing observation made by Laudois (*Virchows Archiv* vol. 35), who thought it was due to an acute generation of gas in the hair. But that such a conspicuous fading of the hair should occur in an inconceivably short time, at least in the course of a few weeks, when the sorrow is extreme, I have myself observed to happen in a few cases.

(10) The Italian physiologist, Mantegazza, relates how, a few years ago, an animal trainer raised great excitement because, after a dangerous fight with a lion that attacked him in the cage, all his hair fell out over night.

A few years ago, it happened in a French town that a young girl, who saved herself in the collapse of a house by clinging to a rafter, lost not only the hair on her head, but also her eye-brows and eye-lashes, in short, all the hairs on her body, within the following few days, (*Cf. Arch. générales de médecine, June 1879, p. 746.*)

Undoubtedly it is easier to explain a sudden falling out of the hair than a sudden turning gray, which plays a certain part in popular imagination and in novels. (*Cf.* Addenda 9.)

The nails, too, are supposed to drop off under the influence of fear, though not as rapidly. (*Cardanus, De subtilitate, lib. XV.*)

(11) That fright can, according to its degree, produce either an increase or a paralysis of the activity of the heart, is not difficult to explain physiologically; at least, this holds true for that conception according to which the vagus nerve acts as the motor nerve for the

heart and possesses the power of causing the contractions of the heart to increase at every slight stimulation, no matter of what kind, and to inhibit the contraction at any stronger stimulation.

(12) The involuntary evacuation of the bladder and intestine are, as a rule, described as paralytic phenomena, caused by a paralysis of the sphincter muscles. In another place, I have demonstrated the fallacy of this conception. (*Cf. Hospitals-Tidende 1872, No. 30, J.*, and *Forlaes over Rygm. Patologi, p. 175 ff.*) Besides, De Marées (*l.c.*, p. 370) has come to the conclusion that these phenomena involve a convulsion. In those not rare cases where sudden fear necessitates an evacuation, it can only be a question of a convulsion of those involuntary muscles.

(13) When the sensory elements of one of the nervous centers, the brain or spinal cord, are subjected to stimulation, sensations do not arise at the place of stimulation, but at the peripheral end of the nerve-fiber. This sensation is called eccentric or projected, according to its origin.

(14) Surely it rests upon an illusion to claim to observe a pulsation of this blood-vessel in cases of anger. (Thus the Mohammedans claim that "the great artery in the center of the Prophet's brow beat when he was angry.")

(15) Perhaps we will be asked here whether the above described congestion of the capillaries is not also of a nervous nature and attributable to the same stemming of the blood as the dilation of the larger veins. However, various facts contradict this explanation. On the one hand, a rich blood-supply occurs in anger without showing any dilation of the larger blood-vessels. On the other hand, the skin does not retain its peculiar blue (cyanotic) coloring, which occurs in cases of superfluity of venous blood. Finally, an experiment on turkeys shows that after severing certain nerves, making the active dilation of the blood-vessels in the neck and head impossible, the characteristic high red coloring and the swelling of their beak and throat gills does not take place, even in violent attacks of anger.

(16) It is well known that Darwin made an attempt to demonstrate the theory of evolution in physiognomic expression and in emotional movements. The very entertaining and inspiring book in which he published these observations and theories (*The Expression of Emotions in Man and Animals*) bears, as do all the works from the pen of that great investigator, the stamp of genius and contains a quantity of fine observations and remarks. But his theories in this field are not tenable. It is questionable whether the decided evolutionary tendency which his pioneer researches have imparted to modern, and especially to English, psychology has been fortunate. Surely not in so far as the psychology of the emotions is concerned, for here this tendency has led to a neglect of real physiological

analysis and hence has digressed from the only true way by which Malebranche, Leuhossek, Libbern, and others have tried to reach their aim, and they would have attained it, too, if the essential physiological fact, the vasomotor function, had not been unknown at that time.

(17) By coördination, we mean the distribution of motor impulse, which reaches only those muscles which are requisite to the performance of a certain determined action, and by which the amount of impulse sent to each part is properly regulated. As I have pointed out elsewhere, it is for this reason that coördination is an acquired skill, not a faculty innate in any specific organ of the nervous system as is so frequently assumed. There is one coördination which is active in the brain, another which is situated in the spinal cord. The disturbance in coördination discussed here must proceed probably from the brain. However, I cannot deal with the question in detail here.

(18) Tissot (*Traité des nerfs, T. II, ps. I, p. 358*) contradicts Galen absolutely and offers several partly plausible examples of sudden death due to a violent attack of rage. Brain hemorrhages, however, were the cause of these deaths, and, in the light of our modern knowledge of the causes of apoplexy, we can assume that a predisposition to these was present, even if the congestion due to the emotion did cause the catastrophy.

(19) The phenomenon of incoördination, as considered here, is only to be found in voluntary muscle action. However, a simultaneous analogous uncertainty of vascular innervation may possibly occur with incoördination. Whether anything similar to this takes place in other organs, it is not in my power to state.

(20) So far, I have brought the vasomotor function into opposition with the rest of the nervous activity, essentially in order to simplify the matter. Yet I have not lost sight of the fact that, in the question of the expression of the affection, it may occur to one that the vasomotor apparatus is involved only as a part of the involuntary nerve-muscle apparatus, and that it is the latter which, in emotion, is opposed to the rest of the primarily affected nervous system, so that the disturbances of the bladder and intestinal movements would have to be considered to be primary phenomena. Since this problem cannot yet be decided definitely, and since its solution had no particular significance for our investigation, I shall confine myself to a suggestion of this possibility. On the other hand, I wish to recall the fact that a spasmodic vascular contraction can undoubtedly stimulate the organic muscles to contraction, and also the reflex center for the changes in circulation. Thus we will meet with no difficulty of a physiological nature in tracing the convulsive condition to changes in circulation.

(21) Changes in the blood content of the skin must necessarily be accompanied by variations in the blood supply in the brain and other internal organs. Either the processes in the inner organs are the same as those in the skin, or the vessels in the former do not share in the changes which occur in the innervation of the skin-vessels. In that case hyperaemia in the skin must cause a derived anaemia in the other organs, and conversely anaemia in the skin will result in hyperaemia in the other organs. These latter changes—compared to the secondary ones in the skin—in the blood content, may be very significant, partly because the skin can take up a great deal of blood, and also because it may be deprived of very nearly all its blood as a result of motor effects. Consider, for example the several stages of fever.

(22) It is rather strange that it was possible to establish a complete vaso-motor theory for the bodily expressions of the emotions almost 200 years ago. It was Malebranche, who, in spite of the total absence of any physiological assumptions, knowing nothing of vascular muscles and nerves, was able to recognize the situation. In his famous work *"De la recherche de la vérité"* (1674) he gives an explanation of the part which the heart plays in violent emotions corresponding to the physiology of his time, and then proceeds (*liber V*): "Besides this, there are nerves to the brain for the more rapid and finer regulation of the flow of the essence of life, which surround the arteries of the brain as well as those which lead to other organs.

"This is how it can happen that an unexpected sight or movement in the brain, accompanying any other circumstance, which must modify all the affections, will cause the essence of life to flow to those nerves which surround the arteries. Thus, a contraction of the arteries leading to the brain can cut off the circulation and a dilation can open the way which leads to every part of the body."

"If those arteries which supply the brain are empty, and all other arteries of the body are contracted by these nerves, then the head must be overfilled with blood and the face must be reddened. But if this distribution of blood is changed by a change in the condition of the brain, then the contracted arteries relax and the others contract. Thus the head is emptied of blood, the face turns pale and the slight amount of blood that leaves the heart all streams to the low extremities of the body. The life essence in the brain decreases, and the rest of the body begins to tremble and weaken."

Translated into modern physiological terms, the theory of Malebranche means that every strong emotional impression causes a heightened vasomotor innervation and a contraction of the arteries. If this contraction involves the arteries of the brain, then too little blood reaches the brain, and too much stays in the body. Anemia of the brain leads to general appearances of paralysis. If, on the other hand, in another kind of affection, the head arteries are relaxed, while others are contracted, then brain and face are flooded with blood.

Malebranche's theory necessarily had to be rather vague in view of the time, when nothing was known in physiology about the active changes in caliber of the blood vessels, and did not arouse much notice. Incomplete, as obviously it had to be, and inaccurate in some of the details, nevertheless the theory is very remarkable because of the fact that the originator considered the disturbances of circulation to be the only primary symptoms of the physical concomitants of emotions.

(23) "Man has only one soul, which influences the entire body, and so, if a simple affection directs the whole force of the soul to one point and fills it with ideas and sensations of one kind, then the whole body must share in the expression of this affection and every movement, every member must contribute to it." (*Engle, Ideen zu einer Mimik, Part I, page 310.*) We can hardly wish for a clearer expression of the popular conception that affections are some sort of demons, sometimes good, sometimes bad, which occasionally disturb the soul of man.

(24) I also wish to recall the oft quoted etymology of the word "Angst" according to Max Müller's theory. From the Sanskrit root *ah* or *anh* (to crush, torture, murder) we have the Sanskrit *ahi*, snake—the latin *anguis;* furthermore, the latin *ango*, to compress, frighten and *angor*, which applies to the physical sensation of oppression, contraction of the throat (*angina*) as well as the emotional feeling. From the same root we have the Gothic *ages*, fear, and the English *anguish*, the Germanic *Angst*, the Latin *angustiae*, the French *angoisse*, etc.

(25) Still more instructive are the cases where emotional outbreaks are caused by inadequate stimuli. I have found no reference to this phenomena in other authors, and it seems to be rare; however, I have observed several cases. One of these was a very intelligent man, not at all nervous, whom I was treating with a painful caustic for a small sore on his tongue. Invariably a fit of laughter appeared at the height of this operation, although there was nothing to laugh at. In the case of a lady, who suffered from paralysis of one side in consequence of a brain disease, but whose mental life had not been impaired in the least, she suddenly began to laugh whenever anyone told her a sad or disagreeable tale, although she was not at all humorously affected. It is evident that a case like the latter can contribute greatly to the solution of our problem if it be subjected to a rigorous analysis. Unfortunately, my observations took place at a time when I could not devote myself to their study.

(26) From more recent times, we have experiments of Bechtereff in St. Petersburg (*cf. Neurolog. Centralblatt 1883, No. 4*), in which he believes to have proved that the occipital lobe "involves essentially

the so-called movements of expression and expressive sounds." This surely does not follow from his observations, and might just as well prove that emotions may arise even after the destruction of the hemispheres.

(27) Since sometimes a mere "memory" may call forth an emotion, without any sense-impression, and with only internal brain processes; then the process may for the moment be even simpler than the example quoted in the text. Nevertheless, a process must be presupposed to have happened in the past; a circumstance which has conditioned a permanent change in certain brain cells; and this process must, strictly speaking, be considered an emotional process, even though separated by an interval of time.

(28) I do not know whether a similar conception of the nature of the affections has ever been made before. At least, there are no records of it in scientific physiology. Spinoza approaches it most closely, in so far as he does not make the bodily phenomena in affections dependent upon mental activity, but in that he places them in the same plane as the latter, as is evident from his definition: "*Per affectum intelligo corporis affectiones quibus ipsius corporis potentia augetur, vel mimiturjuvatur, vel coercetur, et simul harum affectionem ideas.*" (Ethics p. III.) But he pursues the problem no further.

In an Italian book of the last century, which bears the curious title "*Della Fisiinomia, Principi derivati dall' Anatomia, dalla Fisiologia, e Dinamica del corpo umano par mezzo de' quali si distinguono Gli Aristocratici, ed i Realisti dai Democratici di Girolamo Bocalosi, V. ed Milano, Anno VI repubbl.*" However, it has an otherwise very scientific point of view. I found in it (p. 20 f) the following declaration. "*Jo chiamo passione d'un corpo quella tal tendenza e disposizione che hanno le parti componenti, e il tuttinsieme di qualunque corpo a un tale e tal movimento a azione qualunque, dipendente da una causa estrinseca, è per cui quella data azione e necessario effeto di quella tal causa.*"

"*Se questa e la vera definizione delle passioni in genere, noi avremo adesso una limpida idea della parola passione, e vedrassi ora da questo, che dalla tal data organizzazione d'un homo, dalla struttura de' suoi nervi, de suoi vasi, e della tempra ed equilibrio dè suoi umori dee dipender la natura, la diversita e l'energia maggiore o minore delle sue passioni. A parlar dunque propriamente le passioni sono negli organi dell' uomo, e non nello spirito, e così le loro buone o rie qualità, dalla contruzione dipender devono di tuto l'organico, mentre la spirito non sembra che un attributo di quello o se si vuole, ci non agisce che in consequenza della natura e testura dell' organo.*"

The author does not seem to approach very closely the theory which I have set forth here; but the last passage of the quoted abstract, which he does not carry out with more detail, makes his point seem somewhat hazy to me.

THE EMOTIONS

BY

WILLIAM JAMES

THE EMOTIONS[1]

WILLIAM JAMES

[Chapter XXV of the *Principles of Psychology*]

In speaking of the instincts it has been impossible to keep them separate from the emotional excitements which go with them. Objects of rage, love, fear, etc., not only prompt a man to outward deeds, but provoke characteristic alterations in his attitude and visage, and affect his breathing, circulation, and other organic functions in specific ways. When the outward deeds are inhibited, these latter emotional expressions still remain, and we read the anger in the face, though the blow may not be struck, and the fear betrays itself in voice and color, though one may suppress all other sign. *Instinctive reactions and emotional expressions thus shade imperceptibly into each other. Every object that excites an instinct excites an emotion as well.* Emotions, however, fall short of instincts, in that the emotional reaction usually terminates in the subject's own body, whilst the instinctive reaction is apt to go farther and enter into practical relations with the exciting object.

Emotional reactions are often excited by objects with which we have no practical dealings. A ludicrous object, for example, or a beautiful object are not necessarily objects to which we *do* anything; we simply laugh, or stand in admiration, as the case may be. The class of emotional, is thus rather larger than that of instinctive, impulses, commonly so called. Its stimuli are more numerous, and its expressions are more internal and delicate, and often less practical. The physiological plan and essence of the two classes of impulse, however, is the same.

As with instincts, so with emotions, the mere memory or imagination of the object may suffice to liberate the excitement. One may get angrier in thinking over one's insult than at the moment of receiving it; and we melt more over a mother who is dead than we ever did when she was living. In the rest of the chapter I

---

[1] Parts of this chapter have already appeared in an article published in 1884 in *Mind*.

shall use the word *object* of emotion indifferently to mean one which is physically present or one which is merely thought of.

It would be tedious to go through a complete list of the reactions which characterize the various emotions. For that the special treatises must be referred to. A few examples of their variety, however, ought to find a place here. Let me begin with the manifestations of Grief as a Danish physiologist, C. Lange, describes them:[2]

The chief feature in the physiognomy of grief is perhaps its paralyzing effect on the voluntary movements. This effect is by no means as extreme as that which fright produces, being seldom more than that degree of weakening which makes it cost an effort to perform actions usually done with ease. It is, in other words, a feeling of weariness; and (as in all weariness) movements are made slowly, heavily, without strength, unwillingly, and with exertion, and are limited to the fewest possible. By this the grieving person gets his outward stamp: he walks slowly, unsteadily, dragging his feet and hanging his arms. His voice is weak and without resonance, in consequence of the feeble activity of the muscles of expiration and of the larynx. He prefers to sit still, sunk in himself and silent. The tonicity or "latent innervation" of the muscles is strikingly diminished. The neck is bent, the head hangs ("bowed down" with grief), the relaxation of the cheek- and jaw-muscles makes the face look long and narrow, the jaw may even hang open. The eyes appear large, as is always the case where the *orbicularis* muscle is paralyzed, but they may often be partly covered by the upper lid which droops in consequence of the laming of its own *levator*. With this condition of weakness of the voluntary nerve- and muscle-apparatus of the whole body, there coexists, as aforesaid, just as in all states of similar motor weakness, a subjective feeling of weariness and heaviness, of something which weighs upon one; one feels "downcast," "oppressed," "laden," one speaks of his "weight of sorrow," one must "bear up" under it, just as one must "keep down" his anger. Many there are who "succumb" to sorrow to such a degree that they literally cannot stand upright, but sink or lean against surrounding objects, fall on their knees, or, like Romeo in the monk's cell, throw themselves upon the earth in their despair.

But this weakness of the entire voluntary motor apparatus (the so-called apparatus of "animal" life) is only one side of the physiology of grief. Another side, hardly less important, and in its consequences perhaps even more so, belongs to another subdivision of the motor apparatus, namely, the involuntary or "organic" muscles, especially those which are found in

---

[2] Ueber Gemüthsbewegungen, uebersetzt von H. Kurella (Leipzig, 1887).

the walls of the blood-vessels, and the use of which is, by contracting, to diminish the latter's calibre. These muscles and their nerves, forming together the "vaso-motor apparatus," act in grief contrarily to the voluntary motor apparatus. Instead of being paralyzed, like the latter, the vascular muscles are more strongly contracted than usual, so that the tissues and organs of the body become anæmic. The immediate consequence of this bloodlessness is pallor and shrunkenness, and the pale color and collapsed features are the peculiarities which, in connection with the relaxation of the visage, give to the victim of grief his characteristic physiognomy, and often give an impression of emaciation which ensues too rapidly to be possibly due to real disturbance of nutrition, or waste uncompensated by repair. Another regular consequence of the bloodlessness of the skin is a feeling of cold, and shivering. A constant symptom of grief is sensitiveness to cold, and difficulty in keeping warm. In grief, the inner organs are unquestionably anæmic as well as the skin. This is of course not obvious to the eye, but many phenomena prove it. Such is the diminution of the various secretions, at least of such as are accessible to observation. The mouth grows dry, the tongue sticky, and a bitter taste ensues which it would appear, is only a consequence of the tongue's dryness. [The expression "bitter sorrow" may possibly arise from this.] In nursing women the milk diminishes or altogether dries up. There is one of the most regular manifestations of grief, which apparently contradicts these other physiological phenomena, and that is the weeping, with its profuse secretion of tears, its swollen reddened face, red eyes, and augmented secretion from the nasal mucous membrane.

Lange goes on to suggest that this may be a reaction from a previously contracted vaso-motor state. The explanation seems a forced one. The fact is that there are changeable expressions of grief. The weeping is as apt as not to be immediate, especially in women and children. Some men can never weep. The tearful and the dry phases alternate in all who can weep, sobbing storms being followed by periods of calm; and the shrunken, cold and pale condition which Lange describes so well is more characteristic of a severe settled sorrow than of an acute mental pain. Properly we have two distinct emotions here, both prompted by the same object, it is true, but affecting different persons, or the same person at different times, and *feeling* quite differently whilst they last, as anyone's consciousness will testify. There is an excitment during the crying fit which is not without a certain pungent pleasure of its own; but it would take a genius for felicity to discover any dash of redeeming quality in the feeling of dry and shrunken sorrow.—Our author continues:

If the smaller vessels of the lungs contract so that these organs become anæmic, we have (as is usual under such conditions) the feeling of insufficient breath, and of oppression of the chest, and these tormenting sensations increase the sufferings of the griever, who seeks relief by long-drawn sighs, instinctively, like every one who lacks breath from whatever cause.[3]

The anæmia of the brain in grief is shown by intellectual inertia, dullness, a feeling of mental weariness, effort, and indisposition to work, often by sleeplessness. Indeed it is the anæmia of the motor centres of the brain which lies at the bottom of all that weakening of the voluntary powers of motion which we described in the first instance.

My impression is that Dr. Lange simplifies and universalizes the phenomena a little too much in this description, and in particular that he very likely overdoes the anæmia business. But such as it is, his account may stand as a favorable specimen of the sort of descriptive work to which the emotions have given rise.

Take next another emotion, Fear, and read what Mr. Darwin says of its effects:

Fear is often preceded by astonishment, and is so far akin to it that both lead to the senses of sight and hearing being instantly aroused. In both cases the eyes and mouth are widely opened and the eyebrows raised.

---

[3] The bronchial tubes may be contracted as well as the ramifications of the pulmonary artery. Professor J. Henle has, amongst his Anthropologische Vorträge, an exquisite one on the "National History of the Sigh," in which he represents our inspirations as the result of a battle between the red muscles of our skeleton, ribs, and diaphragm, and the white ones of the lungs, which seek to narrow the calibre of the air-tubes. "In the normal state the former easily conquer, but under other conditions they either conquer with difficulty or are defeated. . . . . The contrasted emotions express themselves in similarly contrasted wise, by spasm and paralysis of the unstriped muscles, and for the most part alike in all the organs which are provided with them, as arteries, skin, and bronchial tubes. The contrast among the emotions is generally expressed by dividing them into exciting and depressing ones. It is a remarkable fact that the depressing emotions, like fear, horror, disgust, increase the contraction of these smooth muscles, whilst the exciting emotions, like joy, anger, etc., make them relax. Contrasts of temperature act similarly, cold like the depressing, and warmth like the exciting, emotions. Cold produces pallor and goose-flesh, warmth smooths out the skin and widens the vessels. If one notices the uncomfortable mood brought about by strained expectation, anxiety before a public address, vexation at an unmerited affront, etc., one finds that the suffering part of it concentrates itself principally in

The frightened man at first stands like a statue, motionless and breathless, or crouches down as if instinctively to escape observation. The heart beats quickly and violently, so that it palpitates or knocks against the ribs; but it is very doubtful if it then works more efficiently than usual, so as to send a greater supply of blood to all parts of the body; for the skin instantly becomes pale as during incipient faintness. This paleness of the surface, however, is probably in large part, or is exclusively, due to the vaso-motor centre being affected in such a manner as to cause the contraction of the small arteries of the skin. That the skin is much affected under the sense of great fear, we see in the marvellous manner in which perspiration immediately exudes from it. This exudation is all the more remarkable, as the surface is then cold, and hence the term, a cold sweat; whereas the sudorific glands are properly excited into action when the surface is heated. The hairs also on the skin stand erect, and the superficial muscles shiver. In connection with the disturbed action of the heart the breathing is hurried. The salivary glands act imperfectly; the mouth becomes dry and is often opened and shut. I have also noticed that under slight fear there is strong tendency to yawn. One of the best marked symptoms is the trembling of all the muscles of the body; and this is often first seen in the lips. From this cause, and from the dryness of the mouth, the voice becomes husky or indistinct or may altogether fail. "Obstupui steteruntque comæ, et vox faucibus hæsit." . . . . As fear increases into an agony of terror, we behold, as under all violent emotions, diversi-

---

the chest, and that it consists in a soreness, hardly to be called pain, felt in the middle of the breast and due to an unpleasant resistance which is offered to the movements of inspiration, and sets a limit to their extent. The insufficiency of the diaphragm is obtruded upon consciousness, and we try by the aid of the external voluntary chest-muscles to draw a deeper breath. [This is the sigh.] If we fail, the unpleasantness of the situation is increased, for then to our mental distress is added the corporeally repugnant feeling of lack of air, a slight degree of suffocation. If, on the contrary, the outer muscles overcome the resistance of the inner ones, the oppressed breast is lightened. We think we speak symbolically when we speak of a stone weighing on our heart, or of a burden rolled from off our breast. But really we only express the exact fact for we should have to raise the entire weight of the atmosphere (about 820 kilog.) at each inspiration, if the air did not balance it by streaming into our lungs" (p. 55). It must not be forgotten that an inhibition of the inspiratory centre similar to that produced by exciting the superior laryngeal nerve may possibly play a part in these phenomena. For a very interesting discussion of the respiratory difficulty and its connection with anxiety and fear see "A Case of Hydrophobia," by the lamented Thomas B. Curtis in the *Boston Med. and Surg. Journal*, November 7 and 14, 1878, and remarks thereon by James J. Putnam, *ibid*, November 21.

fied results. The heart beats wildly or must fail to act and faintness ensues; there is a death-like pallor; the breathing is labored; the wings of the nostrils are widely dilated; there is a gasping and convulsive motion of the lips, a tremor on the hollow cheek, a gulping and catching of the throat; the uncovered and protruding eyeballs are fixed on the object of terror; or they may roll restlessly from side to side, *huc illuc volens oculos totumque pererrat*. The pupils are said to be enormously dilated. All the muscles of the body may become rigid or may be thrown into convulsive movements. The hands are alternately clenched and opened, often with a twitching movement. The arms may be protruded as if to avert some dreadful danger, or may be thrown wildly over the head. The Rev. Mr. Hagenauer has seen this latter action in a terrified Australian. In other cases there is a sudden and uncontrollable tendency to headlong flight; and so strong is this that the boldest soldiers may be seized with a sudden panic.[4]

Finally take Hatred, and read the synopsis of its possible effects as given by Sig. Mantegazza:[5]

Withdrawal of the head backwards, withdrawal of the trunk; projection forwards of the hands, as if to defend one's self against the hated object; contraction or closure of the eyes; elevation of the upper lip and closure of the nose,—these are all elementary movements of turning away. Next threatening movements, as: intense frowning; eyes wide open; display of teeth; grinding teeth and contracting jaws; opened mouth with tongue advanced; clenched fists; threatening action of arms; stamping with the feet; deep inspirations—panting; growling and various cries; automatic repetition of one word or syllable; sudden weakness and trembling of voice; spitting. Finally, various miscellaneous reactions and vaso-motor symptoms: general trembling; convulsions of lips and facial muscles, of limbs and of trunk; acts of violence to one's self, as biting fist or nails; sardonic laughter; bright redness of face; sudden pallor of face; extreme dilatation of nostrils; standing up of hair on head.

Were we to go through the whole list of emotions which have been named by men, and study their organic manifestations, we should but ring the changes on the elements which these three typical cases involve. Rigidity of this muscle, relaxation of that, constriction of arteries here, dilatation there, breathing of this sort or that, pulse slowing or quickening, this gland secreting and that one dry, etc., etc. We should, moreover, find that our descriptions had no absolute truth; that they only applied to the

[4] *Origin of the Emotions*, Darwin, pp. 290-2
[5] *La Physionomie et l'Expression des Sentiments* (Paris, 1885), p. 140.

average man; that every one of us, almost, has some personal idiosyncrasy of expression, laughing or sobbing differently from his neighbor, or reddening or growing pale where others do not. We should find a like variation in the objects which excite emotion in different persons. Jokes at which one explodes with laughter nauseate another, and seem blasphemous to a third; and occasions which overwhelm me with fear or bashfulness are just what give you the full sense of ease and power. The internal shadings of emotional feeling, moreover, merge endlessly into each other. Language has discriminated some of them, as hatred, antipathy, animosity, dislike, aversion, malice, spite, vengefulness, abhorrence, etc., etc.; but in the dictionaries of synonyms we find these feelings distinguished more by their severally appropriate objective stimuli than by their conscious or subjective tone.

The result of all this flux is that the merely descriptive literature of the emotions is one of the most tedious parts of psychology. And not only is it tedious, but you feel that its subdivisions are to a great extent either fictitious or unimportant, and that its pretences to accuracy are a sham. But unfortunately there is little psychological writing about the emotions which is not merely descriptive. As emotions are described in novels, they interest us, for we are made to share them. We have grown acquainted with the concrete objects and emergencies which call them forth and any knowing touch of introspection which may grace the page meets with a quick and feeling response. Confessedly literary works of aphoristic philosophy also flash lights into our emotional life, and give us a fitful delight. But as far as "scientific psychology" of the emotions goes, I may have been surfeited by too much reading of classic works on the subject, but I should as lief read verbal descriptions of the shapes of the rocks on a New Hampshire farm as toil through them again. They give one nowhere a central point of view, or a deductive or generative principle. They distinguish and refine and specify *in infinitum* without ever getting on to another logical level. Whereas the beauty of all truly scientific work is to get to ever deeper levels. Is there no way out from this level of individual description in the case of the emotions? I believe there is a way out, but I fear that few will take it.

The trouble with the emotions in psychology is that they are regarded too much as absolutely individual things. So long as they are set down as so many eternal and sacred psychic entities, like the old immutable species in natural history, so long all that *can* be done with them is reverently to catalogue their separate characters, points, and effects. But if we regard them as products of more general causes (as "species" are now regarded as products of heredity and variation), the mere distinguishing and cataloguing becomes of subsidiary importance. Having the goose which lays the golden eggs, the description of each egg already laid is a minor matter. Now the general causes of the emotions are indubitably physiological. Prof. C. Lange, of Copenhagen, in the pamphlet from which I have already quoted, published in 1885 a physiological theory of their constitution and conditioning, which I had already broached the previous year in an article in *Mind*. None of the criticisms which I have heard of it have made me doubt its essential truth. I will therefore devote the next few pages to explaining what it is. I shall limit myself in the first instance to what may be called the *coarser* emotions, grief, fear, rage, love, in which every one recognizes a strong organic reverberation, and afterwards speak of the *subtler* emotions, or of those whose organic reverberation is less obvious and strong.

EMOTION FOLLOWS UPON THE BODILY EXPRESSION IN THE COARSER EMOTIONS AT LEAST

Our natural way of thinking about these coarser emotions is that the mental perception of some fact excites the mental affection called the emotion, and that this latter state of mind gives rise to the bodily expression. My theory, on the contrary, is that *the bodily changes follow directly the perception of the exciting fact, and that our feeling of the same changes as they occur is the emotion.* Common-sense says, we lose our fortune, are sorry and weep; we meet a bear, are frightened and run; we are insulted by a rival, are angry and strike. The hypothesis here to be defended says that this order of sequence is incorrect, that the one mental state is not immediately induced by the other, that the bodily manifestations must first be interposed between, and that the more rational statement is that we feel sorry because we cry, angry because we strike, afraid because we tremble, and not that we cry, strike, or tremble, because we are sorry, angry, or fearful, as the case may be.   Without the bodily states following on the perception, the latter would be purely cognitive in form, pale, colorless, destitute of emotional warmth.   We might then see the bear, and judge it best to run, receive the insult and deem it right to strike, but we should not actually *feel* afraid or angry.

Stated in this crude way, the hypothesis is pretty sure to meet with immediate disbelief.   And yet neither many nor far-fetched considerations are required to mitigate its paradoxical character, and possibly to produce conviction of its truth.

To begin with, no reader of the last two chapters* will be inclined to doubt the fact that *objects do excite bodily changes* by a preorganized mechanism, or the farther fact that *the changes are so indefinitely numerous and subtle that the entire organism may be called a sounding-board*, which every change of consciousness, however slight, may make reverberate.   The various permutations and combinations of which these organic activities are susceptible make it abstractly possible that no shade of emotion, however slight, should be without a bodily reverberation as unique, when taken in its totality, as is the mental mood itself.   The immense number of parts modified in each emotion is what makes it so difficult for us to reproduce in cold blood the total and integral expression of any one of them.   We may catch the trick with the voluntary muscles, but fail with the skin, glands, heart, and other viscera.   Just as an artificially imitated sneeze lacks something of the reality, so the attempt to imitate an emotion in the absence of its normal instigating cause is apt to be rather "hollow."

The next thing to be noticed is this, that *every one of the bodily changes, whatsoever it be, is* FELT, *acutely or obscurely, the moment it occurs.*   If the reader has never paid attention to this matter, he will be both interested and astonished to learn how many different local bodily feelings he can detect in himself as characteristic of his various emotional moods.   It would be perhaps too much to expect him to arrest the tide of any strong gust of pas-

* The chapters on The Production of Movement and on Instinct are in the *Principles.*—[Ed.]

sion for the sake of any such curious analysis as this; but he can observe more tranquil states, and that may be assumed here to be true of the greater which is shown to be true of the less. Our whole cubic capacity is sensibly alive; and each morsel of it contributes its pulsations of feeling, dim or sharp, pleasant, painful, or dubious, to that sense of personality that every one of us unfailingly carries with him. It is surprising what little items give accent to these complexes of sensibility. When worried by any slight trouble, one may find that the focus of one's bodily consciousness is the contraction, often quite inconsiderable, of the eyes and brows. When momentarily embarrassed, it is something in the pharynx that compels either a swallow, a clearing of the throat, or a slight cough; and so on for as many more instances as might be named. Our concern here being with the general view rather than with the details, I will not linger to discuss these, but, assuming the point admitted that every change that occurs must be felt, I will pass on.

I now proceed to urge the vital point of my whole theory, which is this: *If we fancy some strong emotion, and then try to abstract from our consciousness of it all the feelings of its bodily symptoms, we find we have nothing left behind,* no "mind-stuff" out of which the emotion can be constituted, and that a cold and neutral state of intellectual perception is all that remains. It is true that, although most people when asked say that their introspection verifies this statement, some persist in saying theirs does not. Many cannot be made to understand the question. When you beg them to imagine away every feeling of laughter and of tendency to laugh from their consciousness of the ludicrousness of an object, and then to tell you what the feeling of its ludicrousness would be like, whether it be anything more than the perception that the object belongs to the class "funny," they persist in replying that the thing proposed is a physical impossibility, and that they always *must* laugh if they see a funny object. Of course the task proposed is not the practical one of seeing a ludicrous object and annihilating one's tendency to laugh. It is the purely speculative one of subtracting certain elements of feeling from an emotional state supposed to exist in its fulness, and saying what the residual elements are. I cannot help thinking that all who rightly apprehend this problem will agree with the proposition above laid down. What kind of an emotion of fear would be left if the feeling neither of quickened heart-beats nor of shallow breathing, neither of trembling lips nor of weakened limbs, neither of goose-flesh nor of visceral stirrings, were present, it is quite impossible for me to think. Can one fancy the state of rage and picture no ebullition in the chest, no flushing of the face, no dilatation of the nostrils, no clenching of the teeth, no impulse to vigorous action, but in their stead limp muscles, calm breathing, and a placid face? The present writer, for one, certainly cannot. The rage is as completely evaporated as the sensation of its so-called manifestations, and the only thing that can possibly be supposed to take its place is some cold-blooded and dispassionate judicial sentence, confined entirely to the intellectual realm, to the effect that a certain person or persons merit chastisement for their sins. In like manner of grief: what would it be without its tears, its sobs, its suffocation of the heart, its pang in the breast-bone? A feelingless cognition that certain circumstances are deplorable, and nothing more. Every passion in turn tells the same story. A purely disembodied human emotion is a nonentity. I do not say that it is a contradiction in the nature of things, or that pure spirits are necessarily condemned to cold intellectual lives; but I say that for *us*, emotion dissociated from all bodily feeling is inconceivable. The more closely I scrutinize my states, the more persuaded I become that whatever moods, affections, and passions I have are in very truth constituted by, and made up of, those bodily changes which we ordinarily call their expression or consequence; and the more it seems to me that if I were to become corporeally anæsthetic, I should be excluded from the life of the affections, harsh and tender alike, and drag out an existence of merely cognitive or intellectual form. Such an existence, although it seems to have been the ideal of ancient sages, is too apathetic to be keenly sought after by those born after the revival of the worship of sensibility, a few generations ago.

Let not this view be called materialistic. It is neither more nor less materialistic than any other view which says that our emotions are conditioned by nervous processes. No reader of this book is likely to rebel against such a saying so long as it is expressed in general terms; and if any one still finds materialism in the thesis now defended, that must be because of the special processes invoked. They are *sensational* processes, processes due to inward currents set up by physical happenings. Such processes have, it is true, always been regarded by the platonizers in psychology as having something peculiarly base about them. But our emotions must always be *inwardly* what they are, whatever be the physiological ground of their apparition. If they are deep, pure, worthy, spiritual facts on any conceivable theory of their physiological source, they remain no less deep, pure, spiritual, and worthy of regard on this present sensational theory. They carry their own inner measure of worth with them; and it is just as logical to use the present theory of the emotions for proving that sensational processes need not be vile and material, as to use their vileness and materiality as a proof that such a theory cannot be true.

If such a theory is true, then each emotion is the resultant of a sum of elements, and each element is caused by a physiological process of a sort already well known. The elements are all organic changes, and each of them is the reflex effect of the exciting object. Definite questions now immediately arise—questions very different from those which were the only possible ones without this view. Those were questions of classification: "Which are the proper genera of emotion, and which the species under each?" or of description: "By what expression is each emotion characterized?" The questions now are *causal:* "Just what changes does this object and what changes does that object excite?" and "How come they to excite these particular changes and not others?" We step from a superficial to a deep order of inquiry. Classification and description are the lowest stage of science. They sink into the background the moment questions of genesis are formulated, and remain important only so far as they facilitate our answering these. Now the moment the genesis of an emotion is accounted for, as the arousal by an object of a lot of reflex acts which are forthwith felt, *we immediately see why there is no limit to the number of possible different emotions which may exist, and why the emotions of different individuals may vary indefinitely*, both as to their constitution and as to objects which call them forth. For there is nothing sacramental or eternally fixed in reflex action. Any sort of reflex effect is possible, and reflexes actually vary indefinitely, as we know.

We have all seen men dumb, instead of talkative, with joy; we have seen fright drive the blood into the head of its victim, instead of making him pale; we have seen grief run restlessly about lamenting, instead of sitting bowed down and mute; etc., etc.; and this naturally enough, for one and the same cause can work differently on different men's blood-vessels (since these do not always react alike), whilst moreover the impulse on its way through the brain to the vaso-motor centre is differently influenced by different earlier impressions in the form of recollections or associations of ideas.[6]

In short, *any classification of the emotions is seen to be as true and as "natural" as any other*, if it only serves some purpose; and such a question as "What is the 'real' or 'typical' expression of anger, or fear?" is seen to have no objective meaning at all. Instead of it we now have the question as to how any given "expression" of anger or fear may have come to exist; and that is a real question of physiological mechanics on the one hand, and of history on the other, which (like all real questions) is in essence answerable, although the answer may be hard to find. On a later page I shall mention the attempts to answer it which have been made.

DIFFICULTY OF TESTING THE THEORY EXPERIMENTALLY

I have thus fairly propounded what seems to me the most fruitful way of conceiving of the emotions. It must be admitted that it is so far only a hypothesis, only *possibly* a true conception, and that much is lacking to its definitive proof. The only way coercively to *dis*prove it, however, would be to take some emotion, and then exhibit qualities of feeling in it which should be *demonstrably* additional to all those which could possibly be derived from the organs affected at the time. But to detect with certainty such purely spiritual qualities of feeling would obviously be a task beyond human power. We have, as Professor Lange says, absolutely no immediate criterion by which to distinguish

[6] Lange, *op. cit.*, p. 75.

between spiritual and corporeal feelings; and, I may add, the more
we sharpen our introspection, the more *localized* all our qualities
of feeling become and the more difficult the discrimination consequently grows.[7]

A positive proof of the theory would, on the other hand, be
given if we could find a subject absolutely anæsthetic inside and
out, but not paralytic, so that emotion-inspiring objects might
evoke the usual bodily expressions from him, but who, on being
consulted, should say that no subjective emotional affection was
felt. Such a man would be like one who, because he eats, appears
to bystanders to be hungry, but who afterwards confesses that he
had no appetite at all. Cases like this are extremely hard to
find. Medical literature contains reports, so far as I know, of
but three. In the famous one of Remigius Leins no mention is
made by the reporters of his emotional condition. In Dr. G.
Winter's case[8] the patient is said to be inert and phlegmatic, but
no particular attention, as I learn from Dr. W., was paid to his
psychic condition. In the extraordinary case reported by Professor Strümpell (to which I must refer later in another connection)[9] we read that the patient, a shoemaker's apprentice of fifteen,
entirely anæsthetic, inside and out, with the exception of one eye
and one ear, had shown *shame* on the occasion of soiling his bed,
and *grief*, when a formerly favorite dish was set before him, at
the thought that he could no longer taste its flavor. Dr. Strümpell is also kind enough to inform me that he manifested *surprise*,
fear, and *anger* on certain occasions. In observing him, however,
no such theory as the present one seems to have been thought of;
and it always remains possible that, just as he satisfied his natural
appetites and necessities in cold blood, with no inward feeling, so
his emotional expressions may have been accompanied by a quite

[7] Professor Höffding, in his excellent treatise on *Psychology*, admits
(p. 432) the mixture of bodily sensation with purely spiritual affection
in the emotions. He does not, however, discuss the difficulties of discern-
ing the spiritual affection (nor even show that he has fairly considered
them) in his contention that it exists.

[8] *Ein Fall von allgemeiner Anaesthesie* (Heidelberg, 1882).

[9] Ziemssen's *Deutsches Archiv für klinische Medicin*, xxii, 321.

cold heart.[10] Any new case which turns up of generalized anæsthesia ought to be carefully examined as to the inward emotional sensibility as distinct from the "expressions" of emotion which circumstances may bring forth.

Objections considered

Let me now notice a few objections. The replies will make the theory still more plausible.

First objection. There is no real evidence, it may be said, for the assumption that particular perceptions *do* produce wide-spread bodily effects by a sort of immediate physical influence, antecedent to the arousal of an emotion or emotional idea?

Reply. There is most assuredly such evidence. In listening to poetry, drama, or heroic narrative we are often surprised at the cutaneous shiver which like a sudden wave flows over us, and at the heart-swelling and the lachrymal effusion that unexpectedly

[10] The not very uncommon cases of hysterical hemianæsthesia are not complete enough to be utilized in this inquiry. Moreover, the recent researches, of which some account was given in Chapter IV, tend to show that hysterical anæsthesia is not a real absence of sensibility, but a "dissociation," as M. Pierre Janet calls it, or splitting-off of certain sensations from the rest of the person's consciousness, this *rest* forming the self which remains connected with the ordinary organs of expression. The split-off consciousness forms a secondary self; and M. Janet writes me that he sees no reasons why sensations whose "dissociation" from the body of consciousness makes the patient practically anæsthetic, might not, nevertheless, contribute to the emotional life of the patient. They do still contribute to the function of locomotion; for in his patient L. there was no ataxia in spite of the anæsthesia. M. Janet writes me, a propos of his anæsthetic patient L., that she seemed to "suffer by hallucination." "I have often pricked or burned her without warning, and when she did not see me. She never moved, and evidently perceived nothing. But if afterwards in her movements she caught sight of her wounded arm, and *saw* on her skin a little drop of blood resulting from a slight cut, she would begin to cry out and lament as if she suffered a great deal. 'My blood flows,' she said one day; 'I *must be* suffering a great deal.' She suffered by hallucination. This sort of suffering is very general in hysterics. It is enough for them to receive the slightest hint of a modification in their body, when their imagination fills up the rest and invents changes that were not felt." See the remarks published at a later date in Janet's *Automatisme Psychologique*, pp. 214–15.

catch us at intervals.   In listening to music the same is even more strikingly true.   If we abruptly see a dark moving form in the woods, our heart stops beating, and we catch our breath instantly and before any articulate idea of danger can arise.   If our friend goes near to the edge of a precipice, we get the well-known feeling of "all-overishness," and we shrink back, although we positively *know* him to be safe, and have no distinct imagination of his fall. The writer well remembers his astonishment, when a boy of seven or eight, at fainting when he saw a horse bled.   The blood was in a bucket, with a stick in it, and, if memory does not deceive him, he stirred it round and saw it drip from the stick with no feeling save that of childish curiosity.   Suddenly the world grew black before his eyes, his ears began to buzz, and he knew no more.   He had never heard of the sight of blood producing faintness or sickness, and he had so little repugnance to it, and so little apprehension of any other sort of danger from it, that even at that tender age, as he well remembers, he could not help wondering how the mere physical presence of a pailful of crimson fluid could occasion in him such formidable bodily effects.

Professor Lange writes:

No one has ever thought of separating the emotion produced by an unusually loud sound from the true inward affections.   No one hesitates to call it a sort of fright, and it shows the ordinary signs of fright.   And yet it is by no means combined with the idea of danger, or in any way occasioned by associations, memories, or other mental processes.   The phenomena of fright follow the noise immediately without a trace of "spiritual" fear.   Many men can never grow used to standing beside a cannon when it is fired off, although they perfectly know that there is danger neither for themselves nor for others—the bare sound is too much for them.[11]

Imagine two steel knife-blades with their keen edges crossing each other at right angles, and moving to and fro.   Our whole nervous organization is "on-edge" at the thought; and yet what emotion can be there except the unpleasant nervous feeling itself, or the dread that more of it may come?   The entire fund and capital of the emotion here is the senseless bodily effect which the blades immediately arouse.   This case is typical of a class: where an ideal emotion seems to precede the bodily symptoms, it is

[11] *Op. cit.*, p. 63.

often nothing but an anticipation of the symptoms themselves. One who has already fainted at the sight of blood may witness the preparations for a surgical operation with uncontrollable heart-sinking and anxiety. He anticipates certain feelings, and the anticipation precipitates their arrival. In cases of morbid terror the subjects often confess that what possesses them seems, more than anything, to be fear of the fear itself. In the various forms of what Professor Bain calls "tender emotion," although the appropriate object must usually be directly contemplated before the emotion can be aroused, yet sometimes thinking of the symptoms of the emotion itself may have the same effect. In sentimental natures the thought of "yearning" will produce real "yearning." And, not to speak of coarser examples, a mother's imagination of the caresses she bestows on her child may arouse a spasm of parental longing.

In such cases as these we see plainly how the emotion both begins and ends with what we call its effects or manifestations. It has no mental *status* except as either the vivid feeling of the manifestations, or the idea of them; and the latter thus constitute its entire material, and sum and substance. And these cases ought to make us see how in all cases the feeling of the manifestations may play a much deeper part in the constitution of the emotion than we are wont to suppose.

The best proof that the immediate cause of emotion is a physical effect on the nerves is furnished by *those pathological cases in which the emotion is objectless*. One of the chief merits, in fact, of the view which I propose seems to be that we can so easily formulate by its means pathological cases and normal cases under a common scheme. In every asylum we find examples of absolutely unmotived fear, anger, melancholy, or conceit; and others of an equally unmotived apathy which persists in spite of the best of outward reasons why it should give way. In the former cases we must suppose the nervous machinery to be so "labile" in some one emotional direction that almost every stimulus (however inappropriate) causes it to upset in that way, and to engender the particular complex of feelings of which the psychic body of the emotion consists. Thus, to take one special instance, if inability to draw deep breath, fluttering of the heart, and that peculiar epigastric change felt as "precordial anxiety," with an irresistible tendency to take a somewhat crouching attitude and to sit still, and with perhaps other visceral processes not now known, all spontaneously occur together in a certain person; his feeling of their combination *is* the emotion of dread, and he is the victim of what is known as morbid fear. A friend who has had occasional attacks of this most distressing of all maladies tells me that in his case the whole drama seems to centre about the region of the heart and respiratory apparatus, that his main effort during the attacks is to get control of his inspirations and to slow his heart, and that the moment he attains to breathing deeply and to holding himself erect, the dread, *ipso facto*, seems to depart.[12]

The emotion here is nothing but the feeling of a bodily state, and it has a purely bodily cause.

All physicians who have been much engaged in general practice have seen cases of dyspepsia in which constant low spirits and occasional attacks of terror rendered the patient's condition pitiable in the extreme. I have observed these cases often, and have watched them closely, and I have never seen greater suffering of any kind than I have witnessed during these attacks. . . . . Thus, a man is suffering from what we call nervous dyspepsia. Some day, we will suppose in the middle of the afternoon, without any warning or visible cause, one of these attacks of terror comes on. The first thing the man feels is great but vague discomfort. Then he notices that his heart is beating much too violently. At the same time shocks or flashes as of electrical discharges, so violent as to be almost painful, pass one after another through his body and limbs. Then in a few minutes he falls into a condition of the most intense fear. He is not afraid

---

[12] It must be confessed that there are cases of morbid fear in which objectively the heart is not much perturbed. These, however, fail to prove anything against our theory, for it is of course possible that the cortical centres normally percipient of dread as a complex of cardiac and other organic sensations due to real bodily change, should become *primarily* excited in brain-disease, and give rise to an hallucination of the changes being there,—an hallucination of dread, consequently, coexistent with a comparatively calm pulse, etc. I say it is possible, for I am ignorant of observations which might test the fact. Trance, ecstasy, etc., offer analogous examples,—not to speak of ordinary dreaming. Under all these conditions one may have the liveliest subjective feelings, either of eye or ear, or of the more visceral and emotional sort, as a result of pure nerve-central activity, and yet, as I believe, with complete peripheral repose.

of anything; he is simply afraid. His mind is perfectly clear. He looks
for a cause of his wretched condition, but sees none. Presently his terror
is such that he trembles violently and utters low moans; his body is damp
with perspiration; his mouth is perfectly dry; and at this stage there are
no tears in his eyes, though his suffering is intense. When the climax to
the attack is reached and passed, there is a copious flow of tears, or else a
mental condition in which the person weeps upon the least provocation.
At this stage a large quantity of pale urine is passed. Then the heart's
action becomes again normal, and the attack passes off.[13]

Again:

There are outbreaks of rage so groundless and unbridled that all must
admit them to be expressions of disease. For the medical layman hardly
anything can be more instructive than the observation of such a pathological attack of rage, especially when it presents itself pure and unmixed
with other psychical disturbances. This happens in that rather rare disease named transitory mania. The patient predisposed to this—otherwise an entirely reasonable person—will be attacked suddenly without
the slightest outward provocation, and thrown (to use the words of the
latest writer on the subject, O. Schwartzer, *Die transitorische Tobsucht*,
Wien, 1880), "into a paroxysm of the wildest rage, with a fearful and blindly
furious impulse to do violence and destroy." He flies at those about him;
strikes, kicks, and throttles whomever he can catch; dashes every object
about which he can lay his hands on; breaks and crushes what is near him;
tears his clothes, shouts, howls, and roars, with eyes that flash and roll,
and shows meanwhile all those symptoms of vaso-motor congestion which
we have learned to know as the concomitants of anger. His face is red,
swollen, his cheeks hot, his eyes protuberant and their whites bloodshot,
the heart beats violently, the pulse marks 100–120 strokes a minute. The
arteries of the neck are full and pulsating, the veins are swollen, the saliva
flows. The fit lasts only a few hours, and ends suddenly with a sleep of
from 8 to 12 hours, on waking from which the patient has entirely forgotten what has happened.[14]

In these (outwardly) causeless emotional conditions the particular paths which are explosive are discharged by any and every
incoming sensation. Just as, when we are seasick, every smell,
every taste, every sound, every sight, every movement, every
sensible experience whatever, augments our nausea, so the morbid
terror or anger is increased by each and every sensation which
stirs up the nerve-centres. Absolute quiet is the only treatment

[13] R. M. Bucke: *Man's Moral Nature* (N. Y., 1879), p. 97.
[14] Lange, *op. cit.*, p. 61.

for the time. It seems impossible not to admit that in all this the bodily condition takes the lead, and that the mental emotion follows. The *intellect* may, in fact, be so little affected as to play the cold-blooded spectator all the while, and note the absence of a real object for the emotion.[15]

A few words from Henle may close my reply to this first objection:

Does it not seem as if the excitations of the bodily nerves met the ideas half way, in order to raise the latter to the height of emotions? [Note how justly this expresses our theory!] That they do so is proved by the cases in which particular nerves, when specially irritable, share in the emotion and determine its quality. When one is suffering from an open wound, any grievous or horrid spectacle will cause pain in the wound. In sufferers from heart-disease there is developed a psychic excitability, which is often incomprehensible to the patients themselves, but which comes from the heart's liability to palpitate. I said that the very quality of the emotion is determined by the organs disposed to participate in it. Just as surely as a dark foreboding, rightly grounded on interference from the constellations, will be accompanied by a feeling of oppression in the chest, so surely will a similar feeling of oppression, when due to disease of the thoracic organs, be accompanied by groundless forebodings. So small a thing as a bubble of air rising from the stomach through the œsophagus, and loitering on its way a few minutes and exerting pressure on the heart, is able during sleep to occasion a nightmare, and during waking to produce a vague anxiety. On the other hand, we see that joyous thoughts dilate our blood-vessels, and that a suitable quantity of wine, because it dilates the vessels, also disposes us to joyous thoughts. If both the jest and the

---

[15] I am inclined to think that in some hysteriform conditions of grief, rage, etc., the visceral disturbances are less strong than those which go to outward expression. We have then a tremendous verbal display with a hollow inside. Whilst the bystanders are wrung with compassion, or pale with alarm, the subject all the while lets himself go, but feels his insincerity, and wonders how long he can keep up the performance. The attacks are often surprisingly sudden in their onset. The treatment here is to intimidate the patient by a stronger will. Take out your temper, if he takes out his—"Nay, if thou'lt mouth, I'll rant as well as thou." These are the cases of apparently great bodily manifestation with comparatively little real subjective emotion, which may be used to throw discredit on the theory advanced in the text.—It is probable that the visceral manifestations in these cases are quite disproportionately slight, compared with those of the vocal organs. The subject's state is somewhat similar to that of an actor who does not feel his part.

wine work together, they supplement each other in producing the emotional effect, and our demands on the jest are the more modest in proportion as the wine takes upon itself a larger part of the task.[16]

Second objection. If our theory be true, a necessary corollary of it ought to be this: that any voluntary and cold-blooded arousal of the so-called manifestations of a special emotion ought to give us the emotion itself. Now this (the objection says) is not found to be the case. An actor can perfectly simulate an emotion and yet be inwardly cold; and we can all pretend to cry and not feel grief; and feign laughter without being amused.

Reply. In the majority of emotions this test is inapplicable; for many of the manifestations are in organs over which we have no voluntary control. Few people in pretending to cry can shed real tears, for example. But, within the limits in which it can be verified, experience corroborates rather than disproves the corollary from our theory, upon which the present objection rests. Every one knows how panic is increased by flight, and how the giving way to the symptoms of grief or anger increases those passions themselves. Each fit of sobbing makes the sorrow more acute, and calls forth another fit stronger still until at last repose only ensues with lassitude and with the apparent exhaustion of the machinery. In rage, it is notorious how we "work ourselves up" to a climax by repeated outbreaks of expression. Refuse to express a passion, and it dies. Count ten before venting your anger, and its occasion seems ridiculous. Whistling to keep up courage is no mere figure of speech. On the other hand, sit all day in a moping posture, sigh, and reply to everything with a dismal voice, and your melancholy lingers. There is no more valuable precept in moral education than this, as all who have experience know: if we wish to conquer undesirable emotional tendencies in ourselves, we must assiduously, and in the first instance cold-bloodedly, go through the *outward movements* of those contrary dispositions which we prefer to cultivate. The reward of persistency will infallibly come, in the fading out of the sullenness or depression, and the advent of real cheerfulness and kindliness in

[16] *Op. cit.,* p. 72.—Lange lays great stress on the neurotic drugs, as part of his proof that influences of a physical nature upon the body are the first thing in order in the production of emotions.

their stead. Smooth the brow, brighten the eye, contract the dorsal rather than the ventral aspect of the frame, and speak in a major key, pass the genial compliment, and your heart must be frigid indeed if it do not gradually thaw!

This is recognized by all psychologists, only they fail to see its full import. Professor Bain writes, for example:

> We find that a feeble [emotional] wave . . . is suspended inwardly by being arrested outwardly; the currents of the brain and the agitation of the centres die away if the external vent is resisted at every point. It is by such restraint that we are in the habit of suppressing pity, anger, fear, pride—on many trifling occasions. If so, it is a fact that the suppression of the actual movements has a tendency to suppress the nervous currents that incite them, so that the external quiescence is followed by the internal. The effect would not happen in any case; *if there were not some dependence of the cerebral wave upon the free outward vent or manifestation.* . . . . By the same interposition we may summon up a dormant feeling. By acting out the external manifestations, we gradually infect the nerves leading to them, and finally waken up the diffusive current by a sort of action *ab extra.* . . . Thus it is that we are sometimes able to assume a cheerful tone of mind by forcing a hilarious expression.[17]

We have a mass of other testimony of similar effect. Burke, in his treatise on *The Sublime and Beautiful*, writes as follows of the physiognomist Campanella:

> This man, it seems, had not only made very accurate observations on human faces, but was expert in mimicking such as were in any way remarkable. When he had a mind to penetrate into the inclinations of those he had to deal with, he composed his face, his gesture, and his whole body, as nearly as he could, into the exact similitude of the person he intended to examine; and then carefully observed what turn of mind he seemed to acquire by the change. So that, says my author, he was able to enter into the dispositions and thoughts of people as effectually as if he had been changed into the very men. I have often observed [Burke now goes on in his own person] that, on mimicking the looks and gestures of angry, or placid, or frightened, or daring men, I have involuntarily found my mind turned to that passion whose appearance I strove to imitate; nay, I am convinced it is hard to avoid it, though one strove to separate the passion from its corresponding gestures.[18]

---

[17] *Emotions and Will*, pp. 361-2.

[18] Quoted by Dugald Stewart, *Elements, etc.* (Hamilton's ed.), III, 140. Fechner (*Vorschule der Aesthetik*, 156) says almost the same thing of him-

Against this it is to be said that many actors who perfectly mimic the outward appearances of emotion in face, gait, and voice declare that they feel no emotion at all. Others, however according to Mr. Wm. Archer, who has made a very instructive statistical inquiry among them, say that the emotion of the part masters them whenever they play it well.[19] Thus:

"I often turn pale," writes Miss Isabel Bateman, "in scenes of terror or great excitement. I have been told this many times, and I can feel myself getting very cold and shivering and pale in thrilling situations." "When I am playing rage or terror," writes Mr. Lionel Brough, "I believe I do turn pale. My mouth gets dry, my tongue cleaves to my palate. In Bob Acres, for instance (in the last act), I have to continually moisten my mouth, or I shall become inarticulate. I have to 'swallow the lump,' as I call it." All artists who have had much experience of emotional parts are absolutely unanimous. . . . . "Playing with the brain," says Miss Alma Murray, "is far less fatiguing than playing with the heart. An adventuress taxes the physique far less than a sympathetic heroine. Muscular exertion has comparatively little to do with it." . . . "Emotion while acting," writes Mr. Howe, "will induce perspiration much more than physical exertion. I always perspired profusely while acting Joseph Surface, which requires little or no exertion." . . . . "I suffer from fatigue," writes Mr. Forbes Robertson, "in proportion to the amount of emotion I may have been called upon to go through, and not from physical exertion." . . . . "Though I have played Othello," writes Mr. Coleman, "ever since I was seventeen (at nineteen I had the honor of acting the Moor to Macready's Iago), husband my resources as I may, this is the one part, the part of parts, which always leaves me physically prostrate. I have never been able to find a pigment that would stay on my face, though I have tried every preparation in existence. Even the titanic Edwin Forrest told me that he was always knocked over in Othello, and I have heard Charles Kean, Phelps, Brooke, Dillion, say the same thing. On the other hand, I have frequently acted Richard III without turning a hair."[20]

---

self: "One may find by one's own observation that the *imitation* of the bodily expression of a mental condition makes us understand it much better than the merely looking on. . . . When I walk behind some one whom I do not know, and imitate as accurately as possible his gait and carriage, I get the most curious impression of feeling as the person himself must feel. To go tripping and mincing after the fashion of a young woman puts one, so to speak, in a femine mood of mind."

[19] "The Anatomy of Acting," in *Longman Magazine*, vol. xi, pp. 266, 375, 498 (1888), since republished in book form.

[20] Page 394.

The explanation for the discrepancy amongst actors is probably that which these quotations suggest. The *visceral and organic* part of the expression can be suppressed in some men, but not in others, and on this it is probable that the chief part of the felt emotion depends. Coquelin and the other actors who are inwardly cold are probably able to affect the dissociation in a complete way. Prof. Sikorsky of Kieff has contributed an important article on the facial expression of the insane to the *Neurologisches Centralblatt* for 1887. Having practised facial mimicry himself a great deal, he says:

> When I contract my facial muscles in any mimetic combination, *I feel no emotional excitement*, so that the mimicry is in the fullest sense of the word artificial, although quite irreproachable from the expressive point of view.[21]

We find, however, from the context that Professor S.'s practice before the mirror has developed in him such a virtuosity in the control of his facial muscles that he can entirely disregard their natural association and contract them in any order of grouping, on either side of the face isolatedly, and each one alone. Probably in him the facial mimicry is an entirely restricted and localized thing, without sympathetic changes of any sort elsewhere.

Third objection. Manifesting an emotion, so far from increasing it, makes it cease. Rage evaporates after a good outburst; it is *pent-up* emotions that "work like madness in the brain."

Reply. The objection fails to discriminate between what is felt *during* and what is felt *after* the manifestation. *During* the manifestation the emotion is always felt. In the normal course of things this, being the natural channel of discharge, exhausts the nerve-centres, and emotional calm ensues. But if tears or anger are simply suppressed, whilst the object of grief or rage remains unchanged before the mind, the current which would have invaded the normal channels turns into others, for it must find some outlet of escape. It may then work different and worse effects later on. Thus vengeful brooding may replace a burst of indignation; a dry heat may consume the frame of one who fain would weep, or he may, as Dante says, turn to stone within; and then tears or a

[21] Page 496.

storming fit may bring a grateful relief. This is when the current is strong enough to strike into a pathological path when the normal one is dammed. When this is so, an immediate outpour may be best. But here, to quote Professor Bain again:

There is nothing more implied than the fact that an emotion may be too strong to be resisted, and we only waste our strength in the endeavor. If we are really able to stem the torrent, there is no more reason for refraining from the attempt than in the case of weaker feelings. And undoubtedly the *habitual* control of the emotions is not to be attained without a systematic restraint, extended to weak and strong.

When we teach children to repress their emotional talk and display, it is not that they may *feel* more—quite the reverse. It is that they may *think* more; for, to a certain extent, whatever currents are diverted from the regions below must swell the activity of the thought-tracts of the brain. In apoplexies and other brain injuries we get the opposite condition—an obstruction, namely, to the passage of currents among the thought-tracts, and with this an increased tendency of objects to start downward currents into the organs of the body. The consequence is tears, laughter, and temper-fits, on the most insignificant provocation, accompanying a proportional feebleness in logical thought and the power of volitional attention and decision,—just the sort of thing from which we try to wean our child. It is true that we say of certain persons that "they would feel more if they expressed less." And in another class of persons the explosive energy with which passion manifests itself on critical occasions seems correlated with the way in which they bottle it up during the intervals. But these are only eccentric types of character, and within each type the law of the last paragraph prevails. The sentimentalist is so constructed that "gushing" is his or her normal mode of expression. Putting a stopper on the "gush" will only to a limited extent cause more "real" activities to take its place; in the main it will simply produce listlessness. On the other hand, the ponderous and bilious "slumbering volcano," let him repress the expression of his passions as he will, will find them expire if they get no vent at all; whilst if the rare occasions multiply which he deems worthy of their outbreak, he will find them grow in intensity as life proceeds. On the whole, I cannot see that this third objection carries any weight.

If our hypothesis is true, it makes us realize more deeply than ever how much our mental life is knit up with our corporeal frame, in the strictest sense of the term. Rapture. love, ambition, indignation, and pride, considered as feelings, are fruits of the same soil with the grossest bodily sensations of pleasure and of pain. But the reader will remember that we agreed at the outset to affirm this only of what we then called the "coarser" emotions, and that those inward states of emotional sensibility which appeared devoid at first sight of bodily results should be left out of our account. We must now say a word or two about these latter feelings, the "subtler" emotions. as we then agreed to call them.

THE SUBTLER EMOTIONS

These are the moral, intellectual, and æsthetic feelings. Concords of sounds, of colors, of lines, logical consistencies, teleological fitnesses, affect us with a pleasure that seems ingrained in the very form of the representation itself, and to borrow nothing from any reverberation surging up from the parts below the brain. The Herbartian psychologists have distinguished feelings due to the *form* in which ideas may be arranged. A mathematical demonstration may be as "pretty," and an act of justice as "neat," as a drawing or a tune, although the prettiness and neatness seem to have nothing to do with sensation. We have, then, or some of us seem to have, genuinely *cerebral* forms of pleasure and displeasure, apparently not agreeing in their mode of production with the "coarser" emotions we have been analyzing. And it is certain that readers whom our reasons have hitherto failed to convince will now start up at this admission, and consider that by it we give up our whole case. Since musical perceptions, since logical ideas, can immediately arouse a form of emotional feeling, they will say, is it not more natural to suppose that in the case of the so-called "coarser" emotions, prompted by other kinds of objects, the emotional feeling is equally immediate, and the bodily expression something that comes later and is added on?

In reply to this we must immediately insist that æsthetic emotion, *pure and simple*, the pleasure given us by certain lines and masses, and combinations of colors and sounds, is an absolutely sensationa experience. an optical or auricular feeling that is primary, and not due to the repercussion backwards of other sensations elsewhere consecutively aroused. To this simple primary and immediate pleasure in certain pure sensations and harmonious combinations of them, there may, it is true, be *added* secondary pleasures; and in the practical enjoyment of works of art by the masses of mankind these secondary pleasures play a great part. The more *classic* one's taste is, however, the less relatively important are the secondary pleasures felt to be in comparison with those of the primary sensation as it comes in.[22] Classicism and romanticism have their battles over this point. Complex suggestiveness, the awakening of vistas of memory and association, and the stirring of our flesh with picturesque mystery and gloom, make a work of art *romantic*. The classic taste brands these effects as coarse and tawdry, and prefers the naked beauty of the optical and auditory sensations, unadorned with frippery or foliage. To the romantic mind, on the contrary, the immediate beauty of these sensations seems dry and thin. I am of course not discussing which view is right, but only showing that the discrimination between the primary feeling of beauty, as a pure incoming sensible quality, and the secondary emotions which are grafted thereupon, is one that must be made.

These secondary emotions themselves are assuredly for the most part constituted of other incoming sensations aroused by the diffusive wave of reflex effects which the beautiful object sets up. A glow, a pang in the breast, a shudder, a fulness of the breathing, a flutter of the heart, a shiver down the back, a moistening of the

---

[22] Even the feelings of the lower senses may have this secondary escort, due to the arousing of associational trains which reverberate. A flavor may fairly shake us by the ghosts of "banquet halls deserted," which it suddenly calls up; or a smell may make us feel almost sick with the waft it brings over our memory of "gardens that are ruins, and pleasure-houses that are dust." "In the Pyrenees," says M. Guyau, "after a summer-day's tramp carried to the extreme of fatigue, I met a shepherd and asked him for some milk. He went to fetch from his hut, under which a brook ran, a jar of milk plunged in the water and kept at a coldness which was almost icy. In drinking this fresh milk *into which all the mountain had put its perfume*, and of which each savory swallow seemed to give new life, I certainly experienced a series of feelings which the word *agreeable* is insufficient to designate. It was like a pastoral symphony, apprehended by the taste

eyes, a stirring in the hypogastrium, and a thousand unnamable symptoms besides, may be felt the moment the beauty *excites* us. And these symptoms also result when we are excited by moral perceptions, as of pathos, magnanimity, or courage. The voice breaks and the sob rises in the struggling chest, or the nostril dilates and the fingers tighten, whilst the heart beats, etc., etc.

As far as *these ingredients* of the subtler emotions go, then the latter form no exception to our account, but rather an additional illustration thereof. In all cases of intellectual or moral rapture we find that, unless there be coupled a bodily reverberation of some kind with the mere thought of the object and cognition of its quality; unless we actually laugh at the neatness of the demonstration or witticism; unless we thrill at the case of justice, or tingle at the act of magnanimity; our state of mind can hardly be called emotional at all. It is in fact a mere intellectual perception of how certain things are to be called—neat, right, witty, generous, and the like. Such a judicial state of mind as this is to be classed among awarenesses of truth; it is a *cognitive* act. As a matter of fact, however, the moral and intellectual cognitions

instead of by the ear" (quoted by F. Paulhan from *"Les Problèmes de l'Æsthétique Contemporaine,* p. 63).—Compare the dithyrambic about whiskey of Col. R. Ingersoll, to which the presidential campaign of 1888 gave such notoriety: "I send you some of the most wonderful whiskey that ever drove the skeleton from a feast or painted landscapes in the brain of man. It is the mingled souls of wheat and corn. In it you will find the sunshine and shadow that chase each other over the billowy fields, the breath of June, the carol of the lark, the dews of the night, the wealth of summer, and autumn's rich content—all golden with imprisoned light. Drink it, and you will hear the voice of men and maidens singing the 'Harvest Home,' mingled with the laughter of children. Drink it, and you will feel within your blood the star-lit dawns, the dreamy, tawny dusks of many perfect days. For forty years this liquid joy has been within the happy staves of oak, longing to touch the lips of man."—It is in this way that I should reply to Mr. Gurney's criticism on my theory. My "view," this writer says (*Mind,* ix, 425), "goes far to confound the two things which in my opinion it is the prime necessity of musical psychology to distinguish —the effect chiefly sensuous of mere streams or masses of finely colored sound, and the distinctive musical emotion to which the *form* of a sequence of sound, its melodic and harmonic individuality, even realized in complete silence, is the vital and essential object. It is with the former of these two very different things that the physical reactions, the stirring of the hair—the tingling and the shiver—are by far most markedly connected.

hardly ever do exist thus unaccompanied. The bodily sounding-
board is at work, as careful introspection will show, far more than
we usually suppose. Still, where long familiarity with a certain
class of effects, even æsthetic ones, has blunted mere emotional
excitability as much as it has sharpened taste and judgment, we
do get the intellectual emotion, if such it can be called, pure and
undefiled. And the dryness of it, the paleness, the absence of all
glow, as it may exist in a thoroughly expert critic's mind, not only
shows us what an altogether different thing it is from the "coarser"
emotions we considered first, but makes us suspect that almost
the entire difference lies in the fact that the bodily sounding-
board, vibrating in the one case, is in the other mute. "Not so
very bad" is, in a person of consummate taste, apt to be the highest limit of approving expression. *"Rien ne me choque"* is said
to have been Chopin's superlative of praise of new music. A
sentimental layman would feel, and ought to feel, horrified, on
being admitted into such a critic's mind, to see how cold, how
thin, how void of human significance, are the motives for favor or
disfavor that there prevail. The capacity to make a nice spot

. . . . If I may speak of myself, there is plenty of music from which I
have received as much emotion in silent representation as when presented
by the finest orchestra; but it is with the latter condition that I almost
exclusively associate the cutaneous tingling and hair-stirring. But to
call my enjoyment of the *form*, of the *note-after-note*ness of a melody, a mere
critical 'judgement of right' [see below, p. 472] would really be to deny to
me the power of expressing a fact of simple and intimate expression in
English. It is quintessentially emotion. . . . . Now there are
hundreds of other bits of music . . . which I judge to be *right* without
receiving an iota of the emotion. For purposes of emotion they are to me
like geometrical demonstrations or like acts of integrity performed in
Peru." The Beethoven-rightness of which Gurney then goes on to speak,
as something different from the Clementi-rightness (even when the respective pieces are only heard in idea), is probably a purely *auditory-sensational*
thing. The Clementi-rightness also; only, for reasons impossible to assign,
the Clementi form does not give the same sort of purely auditory satisfaction as the Beethoven form, and might better be described perhaps nega-
tively as *non-wrong*, *i.e.*, free from positively unpleasant acoustic quality.
In organizations as musical as Mr. Gurney's, purely acoustic form gives so
intense a degree of sensible pleasure that the lower bodily reverberation
is of no account. But I repeat that I see nothing in the facts which Mr.
Gurney cites, to lead one to believe in an emotion divorced from *sensational processes* of any kind.

on the wall will outweigh a picture's whole content; a foolish trick of words will preserve a poem; an utterly meaningless fitness of sequence in one musical composition set at naught any amount of "expressiveness" in another.

I remember seeing an English couple sit for more than an hour on a piercing February day in the Academy at Venice before the celebrated "Assumption" by Titian; and when I, after being chased from room to room by the cold, concluded to get into the sunshine as fast as possible and let the pictures go, but before leaving drew reverently near to them to learn with what superior forms of susceptibility they might be endowed, all I overheard was the woman's voice murmuring: "What a *deprecatory* expression her face wears! What self-abne*gation*! How *unworthy* she feels of the honor she is receiving!" Their honest hearts had been kept warm all the time by a glow of spurious sentiment that would have fairly made old Titian sick. Mr. Ruskin somewhere makes the (for him terrible) admission that religious people as a rule care little for pictures, and that when they do care for them they generally prefer the worst ones to the best. Yes! in every art, in every science, there is the keen perception of certain relations being *right* or not, and there is the emotional flush and thrill consequent thereupon. And these are two things, not one. In the former of them it is that experts and masters are at home. The latter accompaniments are bodily commotions that they may hardly feel, but that may be experienced in their fulness by *crétins* and philistines in whom the critical judgment is at its lowest ebb. The "marvels" of Science, about which so much edifying popular literature is written, are apt to be "caviare" to the men in the laboratories. And even divine Philosophy itself, which common mortals consider so "sublime" an occupation, on account of the vastness of its data and outlook, is too apt to the practical philosopher himself to be but a sharpening and tightening business, a matter of "points," of screwing down things, of splitting hairs, and of the "intent" rather than the "extent" of conceptions. Very little emotion here!—except the effort of setting the attention fine, and the feeling of ease and relief (mainly in the breathing apparatus) when the inconsistencies are overcome and the thoughts run smoothly for a while. Emotion and cognition seem then parted even in this last retreat; and cerebral processes are almost feelingless, so far as we can judge, until they summon help from parts below.

NO SPECIAL BRAIN-CENTRES FOR EMOTION

If the neural process underlying emotional consciousness be what I have now sought to prove it, the physiology of the brain becomes a simpler matter than has been hitherto supposed. Sensational, associational, and motor elements are all that the organ need contain. The physiologists who, during the past few years, have been so industriously exploring the brain's functions, have limited their explanations to its cognitive and volitional performances. Dividing the brain division into sensory and motor centres, they have found their division to be exactly paralleled by the analysis made by empirical psychology of the perceptive and volitional parts of the mind into their simplest elements. But the emotions have been so ignored in all these researches that one is tempted to suppose that if these investigators were asked for a theory of them in brain-terms, they would have to reply, either that they had as yet bestowed no thought upon the subject, or that they had found it so difficult to make distinct hypotheses that the matter lay among the problems of the future, only to be taken up after the simpler ones of the present should have been definitively solved.

And yet it is even now certain that of two things concerning the emotions, one must be true. Either separate and special centres, affected to them alone, are their brain-seat, or else they correspond to processes occurring in the motor and sensory centres already assigned, or in others like them, not yet known. If the former be the case, we must deny the view that is current, and hold the cortex to be something more than the surface of "projection" for every sensitive spot and every muscle in the body. If the latter be the case, we must ask whether the emotional *process* in the sensory or motor centre be an altogether peculiar one, or whether it resembles the ordinary perceptive processes of which those centres are already recognized to be the seat. Now if the theory I have defended be true, the latter alternative is all that it demands.

Supposing the cortex to contain parts, liable to be excited by changes in each special sense-organ, in each portion of the skin, in each muscle, each joint, and each viscus, and to contain absolutely nothing else, we still have a scheme capable of representing the process of the emotions. An object falls on a sense-organ, affects a cortical part, and is perceived; or else the latter, excited inwardly, gives rise to an idea of the same object. Quick as a flash, the reflex currents pass down through their preordained channels, alter the condition of muscle, skin, and viscus; and these alterations, perceived, like the original object, in as many portions of the cortex, combine with it in consciousness and transform it from an object-simply-apprehended into an object-emotionally-felt. No new principles have to be invoked, nothing postulated beyond the ordinary reflex circuits, and the local centres admitted in one shape or another by all to exist.

EMOTIONAL DIFFERENCES BETWEEN INDIVIDUALS

The revivability in memory of the emotions, like that of all the feelings of the lower senses, is very small. We can remember that we underwent grief or rapture, but not just how the grief or rapture felt. This difficult *ideal* revivability is, however, more than compensated in the case of the emotions by a very easy *actual* revivability. That is, we can produce, not remembrances of the old grief or rapture, but new griefs and raptures, by summoning up a lively thought of their exciting cause. The cause is now only an idea, but this idea produces the same organic irradiations, or almost the same, which were produced by its original, so that the emotion is again a reality. We have "recaptured" it. Shame, love, and anger are particularly liable to be thus revived by ideas of their object. Professor Bain admits[23] that "in their strict character of emotion proper, they [the emotions] have the minimum of revivability; but being always incorporated with the sensations of the higher senses, they share in the superior revivability of sights and sounds." But he fails to point out that the revived sights and sounds may be *ideal* without ceasing to be distinct; whilst the emotion, to be distinct, must

---

[23] In his chapter on "Ideal Emotion," to which the reader is referred for farther details on this subject.

become real again. Professor Bain seems to forget that an "ideal emotion" and a real emotion prompted by an ideal object are two very different things.

An emotional temperament on the one hand, and a lively imagination for objects and circumstances on the other, are thus the conditions, necessary and sufficient, for an abundant emotional life. No matter how emotional the temperament may be, if the imagination be poor, the occasions for touching off the emotional trains will fail to be realized, and the life will be *pro tanto* cold and dry. This is perhaps a reason why it may be better that a man of thought should not have too strong a visualizing power. He is less likely to have his trains of meditation disturbed by emotional interruptions. It will be remembered that Mr. Galton found the members of the Royal Society and of the French Academy of Sciences to be below par in visualizing power. If I may speak of myself, I am far less able to visualize now, at the age of 46, than in my earlier years; and I am strongly inclined to believe that the relative sluggishness of my emotional life at present is quite as much connected with this fact as it is with the invading torpor of hoary eld, or with the omnibus-horse routine of settled professional and domestic life. I say this because I occasionally have a flash of the old stronger visual imagery, and I notice that the emotional commentary, so to call it, is then liable to become much more acute that is its present wont. Charcot's patient, whose case is given in *Progrès Médical,* 21 juillet, complained of his incapacity for emotional feeling after his optical images were gone. His mother's death, which in former times would have wrung his heart, left him quite cold; largely as he himself suggests, because he could form no definite visual image of the event, and of the effect of the loss on the rest of the family at home.

One final generality about the emotions remains to be noted: *They blunt themselves by repetition more rapidly than any other sort of feeling.* This is due not only to the general law of "accommodation" to their stimulus which we saw to obtain of all feelings whatever, but to the peculiar fact that the "diffusive wave" of reflex effects tends always to become more narrow. It seems as if it were essentially meant to be a provisional arrangement, on the basis of which precise and determinate reactions might arise. The more we exercise ourselves at anything, the fewer muscles we employ; and just so, the oftener we meet an cbject, the more definitely we think and behave about it; and the less is the organic perturbation to which it gives rise. The first time we saw it we could perhaps neither act nor think at all, and had no reaction but organic perturbation. The emotions of startled surprise, wonder, or curiosity were the result. Now we look on with absolutely no emotion.[24] This tendency to economy in the nerve-paths through which our sensations and ideas discharge, is the basis of all growth in efficiency, readiness, and skill. Where would the general, the surgeon, the presiding chairman, be, if their nerve-currents kept running down into their viscera, instead of keeping up amid their convolutions? But what they gain for practice by this law, they lose, it must be confessed, for feeling. For the world-worn and experienced man, the sense of pleasure which he gets from the free and powerful flow of thoughts, overcoming obstacles as they arise, is the only compensation for that freshness of the heart which he once enjoyed. This free and powerful flow means that brain-paths of association and memory have more and more organized themselves in him, and that through them the stimulus is drafted off into nerves which lead merely to the writing finger or the speaking tongue.[25] The trains of *intellectual* association, the

[24] Those feelings which Professor Bain calls "emotions of relativity," excitement of novelty, wonder, rapture of freedom, sense of power, hardly survive any repetition of the experience. But as the text goes on to explain, and as Goethe as quoted by Prof. Höffding says, this is because "the soul is inwardly grown larger without knowing it, and can no longer be filled by that first sensation. The man thinks that he has lost, but really he has gained. What he has lost in rapture, he has gained in inward growth." "It is," as Professor Höffding himself adds, in a beautiful figure of speech, "with our virgin feelings, as with the first breath drawn by the new-born child, in which the lung expands itself so that it can never be emptied to the same degree again. No later breath can feel just like that first one." On this whole subject of emotional blunting, compare Höffding's *Psychologie*, vi. E., and Bain's *Emotions and Will*, chapter iv of the first part.

[25] M. Fr. Paulhan, in a little work full of accurate observations of detail (*Les Phénomènes Affectifs et les Lois de leur Apparition*), seems to me rather to turn the truth upside down by his formula that emotions are due to an inhibition of impulsive tendencies. *One* kind of emotion, namely,

memories, the logical relations, may, however, be voluminous in the extreme. Past emotions may be among the things remembered. The more of all these trains an object can set going in us, the richer our cognitive intimacy with it is. This cerebral sense of richness seems itself to be a source of pleasure, possibly even apart from the *euphoria* which from time to time comes up from respiratory organs. If there *be* such a thing as a purely spiritual emotion, I should be inclined to restrict it to this cerebral sense of abundance and ease, this feeling, as Sir W. Hamilton would call it, of unimpeded and not overstrained activity of thought. Under ordinary conditions, it is a fine and serene but not an excited state of consciousness. In certain intoxications it becomes exciting, and it may be intensely exciting. I can hardly imagine a more frenzied excitement than that which goes with the consciousness of seeing absolute truth, which characterizes the coming to from nitrous-oxide drunkenness. Chloroform, ether, and alcohol all produce this deepening sense of insight into truth; and with all of them it may be a "strong" emotion; but then there also come with it all sorts of strange bodily feelings and changes in the incoming sensibilities. I cannot see my way to affirming that the emotion is independent of these. I will concede, however, that if its independence is anywhere to be maintained, these theoretic raptures seem the place at which to begin the defence.

THE GENESIS OF THE VARIOUS EMOTIONS

On a former page (pp. 453–4) I said that two questions, and only two, are important, if we regard the emotions as constituted by feelings due to the diffusive wave.

(1) *What special diffusive effects do the various special objective and subjective experiences excite?* and

(2) *How come they to excite them?*

uneasiness, annoyance, distress, does occur when any definite impulsive tendency is checked, and all of M. P.'s illustrations are drawn from this sort. The other emotions are themselves primary impulsive tendencies of a diffusive sort (involving, as M. P. rightly says, a *multiplicité des phénomènes*); and just in proportion as more and more of these multiple tendencies are checked, and replaced by some few narrow forms of discharge, does the original emotion tend to disappear.

The works on physiognomy and expression are all of them attempts to answer question 1. As is but natural, the effects upon the face have received the most careful attention. The reader who wishes details additional to those given above on pp. 443-7 is referred to the works mentioned in the note below.[26]

As regards question 2, some little progress has of recent years been made in answering it. Two things are certain:

a. The facial muscles of expression are not given us simply for expression's sake;[27]

b. Each muscle is not affected to some one emotion exclusively, as certain writers have thought.

Some movements of expression can be accounted for as *weakened repetitions of movements which formerly* (when they were stronger) *were of utility to the subject.* Others are similarly weakened repetitions of movements which under other conditions were *physiologically necessary effects.* Of the latter reactions the respiratory disturbances in anger and fear might be taken as examples—organic reminiscences, as it were; reverberations in imagination of the blowings of the man making a series of combative efforts, of the pantings of one in precipitate flight. Such at least is a suggestion made by Mr. Spencer which has found approval. And he also was the first, so far as I know, to suggest that other movements in anger and fear could be explained by the nascent excitation of formerly useful acts.

"To have in a slight degree," he says, "such psychical states as accompany the reception of wounds, and are experienced during flight, is to be in a state of what we call fear. And to have in a slight degree such psychical states as the processes of catching, killing, and eating imply, is to have the desires

---

[26] A list of the older writings on the subject is given in Mantegazza's work, *La Physionomie et l'Expression,* chap. i; others in Darwin's first chapter. Bell's *Anatomy of Expression,* Mosso's *La Paura,* Piderit's *Wissenschaftliches System der Mimik und Physiognomik,* Duchenne's Mécanisme de la Physionomie Humaine, are besides Lange and Darwin, the most useful works with which I am acquainted. Compare also Sully: *Sensation and Intuition,* chap. ii.

[27] One must remember, however, that just in so far forth as sexual selection may have played a part in determining the human organism, selection of expressive faces must have increased the average mobility of the human countenance.

to catch, kill, and eat. That the propensities to the acts are nothing else than nascent excitations of the psychical state involved in the acts, is proved by the natural language of the propensities. Fear, when strong, expresses itself in cries, in efforts to escape, in palpitations, in tremblings; and these are just the manifestations that go along with an actual suffering of the evil feared. The destructive passion is shown in a general tension of the muscular system, in gnashing of teeth and protrusion of the claws, in dilated eyes and nostrils, in growls; and these are weaker forms of the actions that accompany the killing of prey. To such objective evidences every one can add subjective evidences. Every one can testify that the psychical state called fear consists of mental representations of certain painful results; and that the one called anger consists of mental representations of the actions and impressions which would occur while inflicting some kind of pain.''[28]

About fear I shall have more to say presently. Meanwhile the principle of *revival in weakened form of reactions useful in more violent dealings with the object inspiring the emotion* has found many applications. So slight a symptom as the snarl or sneer, the one-sided uncovering of the upper teeth, is accounted for by Darwin as a survival from the time when our ancestors had large canines, and unfleshed them (as dogs now do) for attack. Similarly the raising of the eyebrows in outward attention, the opening of the mouth in astonishment, come, according to the same author, from the utility of these movements in extreme cases. The raising of the eyebrows goes with the opening of the eye for better vision; the opening of the mouth with the intensest listening, and with the rapid catching of the breath which precedes muscular effort. The distention of the nostrils in anger is interpreted by Spencer as an echo of the way in which our ancestors had to breathe when, during combat, their "mouth was filled up by a part of an antagonist's body that had been seized (!)." The trembling of fear is supposed by Mantegazza to be for the sake of warming the blood (!). The reddening of the face and neck is called by Wundt a compensatory arrangement for relieving the brain of the blood-pressure which the simultaneous excitement of the heart brings with it. The effusion of tears is explained both by this author and by Darwin to be a blood-withdrawing agency of a similar sort. The contraction of the muscles around the eyes,

[28] *Psychol.*, §213.

of which the primitive use is to protect those organs from being too much gorged with blood during the screaming fits of infancy, survives in adult life in the shape of the frown, which instantly comes over the brow when anything difficult or displeasing presents itself either to thought or action.

"As the habit of contracting the brows has been followed by infants during innumerable generations, at the commencement of every crying or screaming fit," says Darwin, "it has become firmly associated with the incipient sense of something distressing or disagreeable. Hence, under similar circumstances, it would be apt to be continued during maturity although never then developed, into a crying fit. Screaming or weeping begins to be voluntarily restrained at an early period of life, whereas frowning is hardly ever restrained at any age."[29]

The intermittent expirations which constitute laughter have, according to Dr. Hecker, the purpose of counteracting the anæmia of the brain, which he supposes to be brought about by the action of the joyous or comic stimulus upon the vaso-motor nerves.[30]   A smile is the weak vestige of a laugh.   The tight closure of the mouth in all effort is useful for retaining the air in the lungs so as to fix the chest and give a firm basis of insertion for the muscles of the flanks.   Accordingly, we see the lips compress themselves upon every slight occasion of resolve.   The blood-pressure has to

[29]Weeping in childhood is almost as regular a symptom of anger as it is of grief, which would account (on Darwin's principles) for the frown of anger. Mr. Spencer has an account of the angry frown as having arisen through the survival of the fittest, by its utility in keeping the sun out of one's eyes when engaged in mortal combat(!). (*Principles of Psychology,* II. 546). Professor Mosso objects to any explanation of the frown by its utility for vision, that it is coupled, during emotional excitement, with a dilatation of the pupil which is very unfavorable for distinct vision, and that this ought to have been weeded out by natural selection, if natural selection had the power to fix the frown (see *La Paura,* chap. IX, §vi). Unfortunately this very able author speaks as if all the emotions affected the pupil in the same way. Fear certainly does make it dilate. But Gratiolet is quoted by Darwin and others as saying that the pupils *contract* in anger. I have made no observations of my own on the point, and Mosso's earlier paper on the pupil (Turin, 1875) I have not seen. I must repeat, with Darwin, that we need more minute observations on this subject.

[30]*Physiologie u. Psychologie des Lachens und des Komischen* (Berlin, 1873), pp. 13-15.

be high during the sexual embrace; hence the palpitations, and hence also the tendency to caressing action, which accompanies tender emotion in its fainter forms. Other examples might be given; but these are quite enough to show the scope of the principle of revival of useful action in weaker form.

Another principle, to which Darwin perhaps hardly does sufficient justice, may be called the principle of *reacting similarly to analogous-feeling stimuli*. There is a whole vocabulary of descriptive adjectives common to impressions belonging to different sensible spheres—experiences of all classes are *sweet*, impressions of all classes *rich* or *solid*, sensations of all classes *sharp*. Wundt and Piderit accordingly explain many of our most expressive reactions upon moral causes as symbolic gustatory movements. As soon as any experience arises which has an affinity with the feeling of sweet, or bitter, or sour, the same movements are executed which would result from the taste in point.[31] "All the states of mind which language designates by the metaphors bitter, harsh, sweet, combine themselves, therefore, with the corresponding mimetic movements of the mouth." Certainly the emotions of disgust and satisfaction do express themselves in this mimetic way. Disgust is an incipient regurgitation or retching, limiting its expression often to the grimace of the lips and nose; satisfaction goes with a sucking smile, or tasting motion of the lips. In Mantegazza's loose if learned work, the attempt is made, much less successfully, to bring in the eye and ear as additional sources of symbolically expressive reaction. The ordinary gesture of negation—among us, moving the head about its axis from side to side—is a reaction originally used by babies to keep disagreeables from getting into their mouth, and may be observed in perfection in any nursery.[32] It is now evoked where the stimulus is only an

[31] These movements are explained teleologically, in the first instance, by the efforts which the tongue is forced to make to adapt itself to the better perception or avoidance of the sapid body. (Cf. *Physiol. Psych.*, II, 423.)

[32] Professor Henle derives the negative wag of the head from an incipient shudder, and remarks how fortunate is the abbreviation, as when a lady declines a partner in the ballroom. The clapping of the hands for

unwelcome idea. Similarly the nod forward in affirmation is after the analogy of taking food into the mouth. The connection of the expression of moral or social disdain or dislike, especially in women, with movements having a perfectly definite original olfactory function, is too obvious for comment. Winking is the effect of any threatening surprise, not only of what puts the eyes in danger; and a momentary aversion of the eyes is very apt to be one's first symptoms of response to an unexpectedly unwelcome proposition.—These may suffice as examples of movements expressive from analogy.

But if certain of our emotional reactions can be explained by the two principles invoked—and the reader will himself have felt how conjectural and fallible in some of the instances the explanation is—there remain many reactions which cannot so be explained at all, and these we must write down for the present as purely idiopathic effects of the stimulus. Amongst them are the effects on the viscera and internal glands, the dryness of the mouth and diarrhœa and nausea of fear, the liver-disturbances which sometimes produce jaundice after excessive rage, the urinary secretion of sanguine excitement, and the bladder-contraction of apprehension, the gaping of expectancy, the "lump in the throat" of grief, the tickling there and the swallowing of embarrassment, the "precordial" anxiety" of dread, the changes in the pupil, the various sweatings of the skin, cold or hot, local or general, and its flushings, together with other symptoms which probably exist but are too hidden to have been noticed or named. It seems as if even the changes of blood-pressure and heart-beat during emotional excitement might, instead of being teleologically determined, prove to be purely mechanical or physiological outpourings through the easiest drainage-channels—the pneumogastrics and sympathetic nerves happening under ordinary circumstances to be such channels.

Mr. Spencer argues that the *smallest* muscles must be such

applause he explains as a symbolic abridgment of an embrace. The protrusion of the lips (*der prüfende Zug*) which goes with all sorts of dubious and questioning states of mind is derived by Dr. Piderit from the *tasting* movement which we can see on any one's mouth when deciding whether a wine is good or not.

channels; and instances the tail in dogs, cats, and birds, the ears in horses, the crest in parrots, the face and fingers in man, as the first organs to be moved by emotional stimuli.[33] This principle (if it be one) would apply still more exactly to the muscles of the smaller arteries (though not exactly to the heart); whilst the great variability of the circulatory symptoms would also suggest that they are determined by causes into which utility does not enter. The quickening of the heart lends itself, it is true, rather easily to explanation by inherited habit, organic memory of more violent excitement; and Darwin speaks in favòr of this view (see his *Expression,* etc., pp. 74–5). But, on the other hand, we have so many cases of reaction which are indisputably pathological, as we may say, and which could never be serviceable or derived from what was serviceable, that I think we should be cautious about pushing our explanations of the varied heart-beat too far in the teleological direction. Trembling, which is found in many excitements besides that of terror, is, *pace* Mr. Spencer and Sig. Mantegazza, quite pathological. So are terror's other strong symptoms. Professor Mosso, as the total result of his study, writes as follows:

We have seen that the graver the peril becomes, the more do the reactions which are positively harmful to the animal prevail in number and inefficacy. We already saw that the trembling and the palsy make it incapable of flight or defense; we have also convinced ourselves that in the most decisive moments of danger we are less able to see [or to think] than when we are tranquil. In face of such facts we must admit that the phenomena of fear cannot all be accounted for by "selection." Their extreme degrees are morbid phenomena which show an imperfection in the organism. We might almost say that Nature had not been able to frame a substance which would be excitable enough to compose the brain and spinal marrow, and yet which should not be so excited by exceptional stimulation as to overstep in its reactions those physiological bounds which are useful to the conservation of the creature.

---

[33] *Loc. cit.* §497. Why a dog's face-muscles are not more mobile than they are Mr. Spencer fails to explain, as also why different stimuli should innervate these small muscles in such different ways, if easy drainage be the only principle involved. Charles Bell accounted for the special part played by the facial muscles in expression by their being *accessory muscles of respiration,* governed by nerves whose origin is close to the respiratory centre in the medulla oblongata. They are an adjuvant of *voice,* and like it their function is *communication.* (See Bell's *Anatomy of Expression,* Appendix by Alexander Shaw.)

Professor Bain, if I mistake not, had long previously commented upon fear in a similar way.

Mr. Darwin accounts for many emotional expressions by what he calls the principle of antithesis. In virtue of this principle, if a certain stimulus prompted a certain set of movements, then a contrary-feeling stimulus would prompt exactly the opposite movements, although these might otherwise have neither utility nor significance. It is in this wise that Darwin explains the expression of impotence, raised eyebrows, and shrugged shoulders, dropped arms and open palms, as being the antithesis of the frowning brow, the thrown-back shoulders and clenched fists of rage, which is the emotion of power. No doubt a certain number of movements can be formulated under this law; but whether it expresses a *causal* principle is more than doubtful. It has been by most critics considered the least successful of Darwin's speculations on this subject.

To sum up, we see the reason for a few emotional reactions; for others a possible species of reason may be guessed; but others remain for which no plausible reason can even be conceived. These may be reactions which are purely mechanical results of the way in which our nervous centres are framed, reactions which, although permanent in us now, may be called accidental as far as their origin goes. In fact, in an organism as complex as the nervous system there *must* be many such reactions, incidental to others evolved for utility's sake, but which would never themselves have been evolved independently, for any utility they might possess. Sea-sickness, the love of music, of the various intoxicants, nay, the entire æsthetic life of man, shall have to trace to this accidental origin.[34] It would be foolish to suppose that none of the reactions called emotional could have arisen in this *quasi*-accidental way.

This is all I have to say about the emotions. If one should seek to name each particular one of them of which the human heart is the seat, it is plain that the limit to their number would lie in the introspective vocabulary of the seeker, each race of men having found names for some shade of feeling which other races have left undiscriminated. If then we should seek to break

[34] *La Paura*, Appendice, p. 295.

the emotions, thus enumerated, into groups, according to their affinities, it is again plain that all sorts of groupings would be possible, according as we chose this character or that as a basis, and that all groupings would be equally real and true. The only question would be, does this grouping or that suit our purpose best? The reader may then class the emotions as he will, as sad or joyous, sthenic or asthenic, natural or acquired, inspired by animate or inanimate things, formal or material, sensuous or ideal, direct or reflective, egoistic or non-egoistic, retrospective, prospective or immediate, organismally or environmentally initiated, or what more besides. All these are divisions which have been actually proposed. Each of them has its merits, and each one brings together some emotions which the others keep apart. For a fuller account, and for other classificatory schemes, I refer to the Appendix to Bain's *Emotions and the Will*, and to Mercier's, Stanley's and Read's articles on the Emotions, in *Mind*, vols. IX, X, and XI. In vol. IX. p. 421 there is also an article by the lamented Edmund Gurney in criticism of the view which in this chapter I continue to defend.